Our Thora

Our Thora

Celebrating the First Lady of Showbusiness

Morris Bright

With contributions from
Dame Thora Hird

Hodder & Stoughton

This editon first published in Great Britain in 2002

The right of Morris Bright to be identified as the Author of
the Work has been asserted by him in accordance with the
Copyright, Designs and Patents Act 1988.

10 9 8 7 6 5 4 3 2 1

British Library Cataloguing in Publication Data
A record for this book is available from the British Library

ISBN 0340 78645 0

Printed and bound in Spain

Hodder & Stoughton
A Division of Hodder Headline Ltd
338 Euston Road
London NW1 3BH

Contents

Foreword 7

Acknowledgements 9

Introduction 11

Chapter 1 Film and Theatre 20

Chapter 2 Changing Faces 44

Chapter 3 Television 50

Chapter 4 Family 76

For my son Alexander,
the brightest spark I have ever known.

Foreword

BY ROY CLARKE Writer of *Last of the Summer Wine*

I've never seen Thora walk on and not be instantly convincing. It's not that she persuades us to suspend disbelief. The authority of her performance is such that disbelief never arises. What we see, and immediately, is always exactly the character that she is representing herself to be.

It has been my good luck to have seen her from both sides of the screen. I was always going to be a writer. Where the urge came from I don't know. But it was there already when I was in short pants, which is what we wore in those days when a childhood was still available to children. Your first long pair was a rite of passage – I remember it still and I was scribbling stories in exercise books even then. I'm not claiming I finished them but I was a great starter.

These were the days before television. For a lad in the middle of rural, flat nowhere, the world of entertainment came by radio (unless the battery died) and from cinema. Both seemed fascinating but fairy worlds beyond ordinary human reach. Books on the other hand were familiar. You handled them. You swapped them at school. You lived with them. So I assumed I'd one day be a writer of books.

Those other enchanted and more remote worlds of radio and film I loved purely as a fan. It stayed like that until my thirties. By this time of course I had, along with millions of us, stored in my heart and head that little group of favourite performers who force their way so powerfully into our awareness that they become part of our lives.

What brings them there? Why do they make their mark so strongly? It can't just be the roles they play because we enjoy them in all their roles. It's a quality they bring to every part, however different the characters: a something always shiningly and unmistakably theirs.

Thora came early among these. She brings to the parts she plays not only Thora – and we can't get enough of that – but such a total control of the character that it becomes instantly flesh and bone. The best acting seems not to be acting, which of course it is. For my money, the best acting is that which is so good, it conceals itself by making us accept it as real. We never doubt the reality of a Thora Hird character. It's not even possible. She gives no opportunity to see the joins.

From early days I was a fan of Thora's. I remember being on my honeymoon, watching Thora in the theatre and laughing so excessively my wife was alarmed to be next to this convulsing idiot. And when my writing took me finally into Thora's world, she was still a star on my distant horizon, and I remained a dumbstruck fan, never dreaming she might be coaxed into my orbit.

Happily the producer of *Last of the Summer Wine*, Alan J. W. Bell, has the same admiration for her but much more cheek so, fifteen years ago, Thora joined us and ever since I've had the privilege of writing for this lady who has always so delighted me on stage and screen.

She still does. Ever more so.

I was a fan for years before I met her and it was a delight to find that in that role too, as Thora herself, she gives the same pleasure as she does on stage.

Happily the Thora you see is the Thora you get.

Acknowledgements

Writing and compiling a book on one of this nation's favourite actresses – with a career stretching across almost the entire span of her ninety years – could have proved a daunting task, had it not been for the kind help and assistance offered and provided to me by the following, to all of whom I am deeply indebted:

First and foremost, as if writing a book on Dame Thora Hird were not pleasure enough, I am so truly grateful to both Thora and her daughter Janette for the enthusiastic commitment they have given to this project and for the privilege of not only being welcomed into their homes and private archives – both of memory and photographic stills – but also of having been made to feel one of the family. Our hours together sifting through boxes and boxes of pictures, while Thora recalled so many wonderful stories of yesteryear, were nothing short of a delight and I shall cherish those memories always. It's the most fun I've ever had researching a book.

To do credit to Thora's life stories, research and the quest for historical accuracy are paramount. I therefore extend my thanks to my old chum Robert Ross. Research should be his middle name – the best example of the three R's you could wish for. My thanks also to John Herron and all his colleagues at Canal + Image UK Ltd, whose efforts to help me find stills from as far back as the early 1940s were carried out with a sense of pride and not duty. And to Lois Perry-Smith

for the many tireless hours she spent in the dusty Pinewood archives helping to sift through hundreds of photos with a sense of enthusiasm so remarkable in a woman who wasn't born until Thora Hird was 70!

Thanks also to Peter Wicks and his colleagues at the Pinewood Studios Stills Department, to the BBC Picture Library, PA News Archives, Yorkshire Television and Malcolm Howarth, and especially to Peter Jordan Network Photographers for the stunning shots of Thora's 90th birthday celebrations.

The enjoyment I hope readers will experience by reading Thora's memories of her life can only be enhanced by the memories of those who have lived and worked with her. For their contributions to this book I would like to thank: Roy Clarke, Sir John Mills, Sir Norman Wisdom, Shirley Eaton, Maurice Denham, Frank Thornton, Ronnie Corbett OBE, John Schlesinger, Alan Bates, Kathy Staff, Michael Winner, David Rustidge, Chris Beeny, Alan Plater, Ronald Wolfe, Peter Sallis, Pete Postlethwaite, Deric Longden, Victoria Wood OBE, Dora Bryan, Alan J. W. Bell, Sarah Thomas, Tom Owen, Janette Scott, Daisy Tormé, James Tormé and the late and much-missed Sir Harry Secombe, who even at a time of great illness and pain, picked up the phone to dictate to me his tribute to his lifelong friend Thora for inclusion in this book. They really don't make them like that any more.

My thanks to Judith Longman at Hodder and Stoughton for supporting the project and my ideas from the outset, and her design team for making the words and pictures herein look so wonderful.

And finally to my family who have suffered my long absences from phone and home with much grace. I hope Mum and Dad will now finally forgive me for not becoming a doctor or a lawyer.

Morris Bright

Introduction

Dame Thora Hird is a national institution. As much a part of the British way of life as roast beef for Sunday lunch, rainy bank-holidays and the royal family. Indeed, Dame Thora is often described as the Queen Mother of British entertainment. Fêted by each new generation of actors and directors, she has gone from welcome and beloved comedienne, skilled character actress and, latterly, the face of popular religious broadcasting on BBC television, to the very epitome of the consummate professional. A distinguished and respected actress who has revelled in some of the finest and most poignant dramatic and comic scripts from such master craftsmen of the written word as Victoria Wood and Alan Bennett.

Thora Hird was born on Sunday 28 May 1911 in Morecambe, Lancashire, to the sound of pealing church bells. She was the second of three children to proud parents James Henry and Mary Jane Hird. Her future acting career was almost mapped out for her from the very start. Thora's parents were both theatrical people – they met in a touring company and travelled the entire length of the country on touring seasons that often lasted for months at a time. And while Thora wasn't exactly born between the matinée and evening performances in some small, far-off theatre in some small, far-off town, she did make her first appearance on stage a short while afterwards at the tender age of just eight weeks.

Her mother was appearing in a play as the young heroine whose encounter with the son of the country squire had led to an unfortunate result. Thora played the unfortunate result. She didn't have to audition. Her father was the director and so Thora got the part – the first and last time in her entire career that such influence won her a role.

James Hird became the manager of the Royalty Theatre in Morecambe and with the job came a house. Thora's bedroom floor actually hung over the wall at the back of the stage, and at night she would lie in bed listening to the actors delivering their lines and the reactions of the audience. The theatre, its stage and prop rooms became a playground to Thora and her older brother Neville. They were good times.

As a child, Thora's love of the theatre continued unabated and she was taking on roles from as young as two and playing Morecambe's May Queen by ten. When she was old enough, she joined a repertory company herself but, knowing the precarious nature of the business, kept on her day job at the local Co-op, where she studied the women who came in for their goods. She watched and made a mental note of their voices and characters, their eccentricities and foibles. This was to stand her in good stead when called on to play character roles on both stage and screen. There were to be few actresses who could match Thora's portrayals of dotty chars, scatty maids and frosty landladies, in years to come.

In 1933, the Winter Gardens in her home town of Morecambe was given a complete facelift with copious sums of money spent returning it to its former opulence, reviving its reputation as a first-class variety theatre and ballroom. James Hird was invited to its reopening and took Thora along as his escort. As she sat and watched the show her attention was drawn to the drummer in the orchestra. For the next three years she saw this tall, handsome man every day, before finally marrying him and becoming Mrs James Scott. They lived in their first house – Prompt Corner, Morecambe – which cost the newlyweds the princely sum of £495. In 1938 they had a daughter, Janette, herself to become smitten by the acting bug.

Thora's work in rep continued and gave her the best acting education. It was fun but hard work. In ten years Thora appeared in over five hundred plays, and insisted that she had played a maid so often that she could bring on a tray in at least fifty different ways. Her big break came after she was talent-spotted by an agent for Ealing Film Studios. Thora went to London and auditioned for George Formby. She didn't get the part but was offered a seven-year contract nonetheless, and appeared on the silver screen for the first time in 1941 opposite Will Hay in the corruption-in-high-places comedy thriller, *The Black Sheep of Whitehall*.

Typically, Hay was an incompetent schoolmaster mistaken for a high-flying economics expert. Thora was quite outstanding as Hay's acidic secretary, appearing in the opening sequence and brilliantly undermining his suspect intelligence and dubious correspondence course. It was a small part – just three minutes long – but

Thora made a great impact and thrilled the high and mighty at Ealing Studios who knew that they had been wise to sign her up.

It was with Ealing again that Thora made *The Next of Kin*, an impressively stirring propaganda film. It was so successful that the film enjoyed a commercial release. Her next film, *Went the Day Well?* in 1942, was another cracking Ealing propaganda piece relating the chilling tale of a sleepy English village invaded by fifth columnists and German troops. Told with all the detail and affection of a national outsider (it was directed by the Brazilian Alberto Cavalcanti), Thora scored as the resourceful and plucky telephone switchboard operator. Among the young cast were Ealing stalwart Harry Fowler and Thora's three-year-old daughter Janette Scott. More of the same followed, appearing in Ealing's daredevil *The Foreman Went to France*, with dour Clifford Evans and cheerful Tommy Trinder. The rest of the 1940s saw a spattering of small parts and character roles in various films, notably the grand Herbert Wilcox Victorian melodrama, *The Courtneys of Curzon Street*; Terence Young's creepily effective mystery, *Corridor of Mirrors*; and the suburban romp, *The Weaker Sex*. Thora was ideal for the latter piece, with its larger-than-life characters and post-war satire; one of its immortal lines is, 'Quick, the fishmonger's got fish!'

By the late 1940s Thora was spending more and more of her time away from recently demobbed husband 'Scottie' and daughter Janette, so the family decided it was time to sell their home in Morecambe and move permanently to London. It was difficult tearing themselves away from their roots but

Thora was now the main earner in the family. Scottie agreed that they should concentrate on Thora's burgeoning career and he took on the role of bringing up Janette – which he undertook with great love and pride.

If they had any doubts about the move, these were soon pushed to one side – when Thora's Ealing contract came to an end, she was immediately offered a seven-year contract with J. Arthur Rank. Thora was in great demand. She was building up her roles in British films by day and appearing in successful plays in London by night. It was tiring work, but Thora loved it.

For Rank she appeared opposite Eric Portman in the courtroom drama, *The Blind Goddess* and, later, the Terence Fisher Germanic drama, *Portrait from Life* in a script co-written by Muriel and Sydney Box. She excelled as the down-trodden and emotional mother of Dirk Bogarde's arrogant speedway king in *Once a Jolly Swagman* – made up to look thirty years his senior when in fact their age difference was a mere decade. She slowed down a tad with a featured role in the Honor Blackman and John McCallum cycling club comedy, *A Boy, a Girl and a Bike* before landing a role in the film version of Kenneth Horne's celebrated stage comedy, *Fools Rush In*. Thora joined Margaret Lockwood for the disappointing, pseudo-Rebecca melodrama, *Madness of the Heart*, and then it was back to a flamboyant Herbert Wilcox romance with Anna Neagle and Michael Wilding in *Maytime in Mayfair*, and into the mire and despair of life in Borstal with kindly governor Jack Warner in *Boys in Brown*. This was interesting, if only for a glimpse of future stars making early film appearances, as the cast of teenage

rebels included Dirk Bogarde, Jimmy Hanley and Richard Attenborough. Also in 1949 Thora was rather incongruously cast alongside the 'Taylors' – Robert and Elizabeth – in the Victor Saville-directed romance *Conspirator* for MGM-British, while tackling a further support in the Lancashire-based comedy *The Cure for Love*, starring and directed by the dashing Robert Donat.

At the start of the 1950s, Thora was back at Ealing Studios for her only 'official' Ealing comedy, the mild-mannered and whimsical *The Magnet* directed by Charles Frend. It was to the poverty-row Butchers Films that Thora went next, to appear opposite Pat Kirkwood, Jack Watling and Sydney Tafler in the Lewis Gilbert-directed love triangle drama, *Once a Sinner.* Meanwhile, British Lion cast her in the racehorse syndicate comedy, *The Galloping Major*, featuring a stunning cast of comedy favourites including Basil Radford, Charles Hawtrey and Sid James. Janette Scott, by this time being groomed as one of British film's most talented and attractive stars, played the female lead.

1952 saw Thora take a number of interesting supporting roles, notably in the Dermot Walsh and Barbara Murray drama, *The Frightened Man*, scripted and directed by John Gilling. She featured in the intriguing medical compendium, *Emergency Call*; the hotel-based thriller, *The Lost Hours*; and, most impressively of all, the cheap and cheerful Group 3 rural comedy, *Time Gentlemen Please*, starring Eddie Byrne as a workshy tramp and the only employment blot on the village's copybook. Thora excelled as the cold-hearted and super-efficient charge of the dreary almshouse. Clearly moulded in the great Ealing tradition, Lewis Gilbert was again the director at the helm, while the cast was brought to life by a galaxy of British films' finest, including Sid James, Dora Bryan and Hermione Baddeley.

That veteran director Maurice Elvy dragged Thora, Diana Dors and James Hayter through the comic film, *The Great Game*, relating the sorry tale of a respected football club head getting caught up with a gang of baddies, while Group 3 offered Thora another role in one of her daughter's films, *Background*. Later in 1953 she notched up appearances in the Joan Collins convict drama, *Turn the Key Softly*; the excellent psychological thriller, *The Long Memory* with John Mills; the schoolmaster-attracts-pupil drama *Personal Affair* starring Leon Genn; the Rosamund John police thriller *Street Corner*; and the exhilarating France-day-trip comedy *A Day to Remember* with Stanley Holloway, Donald Sinden and Harry Fowler.

Further low-brow comic credits came along with *Don't Blame the Stork*, *Simon and Laura* and the Dirk Bogarde domestic romance, *For Better, for Worse*. Thora was cast in the memorable department-store, seasonal, sales madness of *The Crowded Day*, scripted by future *Carry On* scriptwriter Talbot Rothwell, but it was with star vehicles that she really found her feet.

In a return to the Will Hay style of comic misadventure, Thora found herself playing opposite Norman Wisdom in the delightful orphanage comedy, *One Good Turn*. One of Norman's best-loved films, the classic train-based sequence with a rogue wasp causing havoc among the passengers is one of the physical comedy classics of British comedy. Again in 1954 Thora

played the long-suffering wife of Arthur Askey in the rollicking film version of Glen Melvyn's footballing stage farce, *The Love Match*. Shirley Eaton was impressive as the daughter of the northern working-class couple, a role that had been taken by Arthur's daughter Anthea on stage.

A dramatic switch came to Thora's film career in 1955 when Val Guest cast her in the classic Hammer science-fiction thriller, *The Quatermass Xperiment*, proudly X-rated even down to the exploitative spelling of the title. *Tiger by the Tail*, based on the novel by RAF war hero John Mair, followed, along with the colourful kidnapping thriller, *Lost. Women without Men* and *Home and Away* were fairly standard dramatic fare before Thora stormed into the blistering comedy, *Sailor Beware*, which gave Peggy Mount her definitive battle-axe persona and Thora another cracking character support. Comic explosion was fast becoming Thora's natural environment.

In January 1956 television producer Ronnie Taylor cast her in the first episode of *Home James* for the BBC, with the gloriously bleary-eyed northern comic Jimmy James rambling through his storytelling and situation comedy, penned by Cass James and Frank Roscoe. Later that year she cropped up as the regular support in the first series of *The Jimmy Wheeler Show* written by Talbot Rothwell and Sid Colin.

As Thora's incredible success flowered on stage and, latterly, on television, she found less and less time for film work. However, in late 1956 she agreed to appear in the remake of *The Good Companions*, starring daughter Janette Scott, as well as in the gritty, Liverpudlian, gangland, Frankie Vaughan musical drama, *These Dangerous Years*. A 1958 short subject, *A Clean Sweep*, pre-empted Thora's return to film comedy when she starred as a flirty passenger aboard Frankie Howerd's jolly ship in Val Guest's nautical romp, *Further Up the Creek*.

The swinging sixties started with a landmark production for Thora when she played the ambitious, corrupted and rather unpleasantly blatant mother of the stunning Shirley Ann Field in Tony Richardson's film version of John Osborne's *The Entertainer*. The potential of a fruitful and degrading relationship with the defeated, depressed and deadening end-of-pier comic of Laurence Olivier brings out Thora's working-class struggle and willingness to agree to anything for her stunning and naïve offspring. Another pivotal kitchen-sink drama from the 'angry young men' movement was the Keith Waterhouse and Willis Hall melodrama, *A Kind of Loving*, with Thora as the resistible mother-in-law from hell opposite that drunken, vomiting 'pig', Alan Bates. June Ritchie was perfectly demure opposite the fiery, powerhouse performance of Thora under the spirited direction of John Schlesinger. The film was a major turning point in Thora's acting career, for while she had played serious dramatic roles on stage, her appearances in film had tended to be dotty or eccentric comedy parts. Even when called on for serious film work, she had never taken the lead role. Suddenly both audiences and film-makers alike saw Thora as a first-class actress.

Thora continued in a serious vein with the Laurence Oliver film, *Term of Trial*, featuring the great actor as a schoolmaster accused of rape, while *Bitter Harvest* traced Janet Munro's unpleasant path of passage from Welsh innocence to corrupted London grime as she unsuccessfully pursued the road of wealth and luxury. *Rattle of a Simple Man*, with Harry H. Corbett, gave Thora more of a comedic chance on the big screen but by that stage she had fully made her mark in her first starring show on television.

Meet the Wife began as a BBC *Comedy Playhouse* pilot in 1963 before its writers, Ronald Wolfe and Ronald Chesney, were commissioned to write a series for broadcast in 1964. The situation was simple: Thora Hird and Freddie Frinton (a legendary stage comedian adept at drunken business) starred as Thora and Freddie Blacklock. Typically, this working-class couple were split by the class struggle, with the husband more than happy with his lot and the wife ferociously trying to better their standing in the community – a 1960s *Keeping up Appearances*. Under the production genius of John Paddy Carstairs (experienced at film comedy with the Norman Wisdom vehicles), Graeme Muir and Robin Nash, the format proved an instant success. With her enforced finery, snobbish values and permanently embittered expression, Thora became a small-screen star, notably turning on the posh accent and invariably addressing her lowly husband as 'Frayd!'. *Meet the Wife* ran to a staggering five series in just under three years, with twelve of its episodes making it into the top twenty most-watched programmes of the week. The show finally came to a close in December 1966. Incidentally, it is the only situation comedy to get a name-check in Beatles' lyrics! In the *Sergeant Pepper* track, 'Good Morning, Good Morning!', John Lennon belts out the line: 'It's time for tea and *Meet the Wife*.'

1966 was a good year all round for Thora. As well as *Meet the Wife* she managed to notch up an even more impressive tally of performances, on stage as well as on television, appearing in *Call My Bluff*, *Dixon of Dock Green*, *The Good Old Days*, *Jackanory*, *Late Night Line Up* and a staggering thirty-two weeks at the London Palladium. It is hardly surprising that she needed a Christmas holiday in Beverly Hills to visit daughter Janette and her second husband, singer Mel Tormé.

Thora returned home early in 1967 and was immediately offered the part of Nurse in BBC TV's *Play of the Month*, *Romeo and Juliet*. She turned it down. Producer Cedric Messina and director Alan Cooke wouldn't accept her refusal. They offered it again and Thora refused it again. A persuasive lunch followed and Thora finally recanted. She was a great success.

In August 1967 Thora started filming *The First Lady*, in which she played a gritty, northern councillor in a gritty, northern town. Initially writer Alan Plater had suggested she should be a renegade in the Labour Party who spent more time fighting with her own colleagues than with the Tories. The BBC hierarchy went a little pale and said: 'We have to be terribly careful about political balance so couldn't she be an Independent?' Which is exactly what happened and Sarah Danby, Independent Councillor for the imaginary northern town of Furness, hit our screens in 1968. The show was a resounding hit and thirty episodes (sadly most of which were wiped in the 1970s) were broadcast over two seasons. Like *A Kind of Loving* before it, *The First Lady* was a turning point in Thora's career, this time bringing her acting abilities to a huge television audience previously used to seeing her performing only knockabout antics in, say, *Meet the Wife*, on the small screen.

Thora followed up this success with a return to television comedy in *Ours is a Nice House* in the starring role of Thora Parker, the sharp-tongued owner of a Lancashire boarding-house who, being widowed, faces the prospect of looking after her two children, Alan and Vera, played by Leslie Meadows and Caroline Dowdeswell. Written by Harry Littlewood and produced by Stuart Allen, two series were broadcast, in 1969 and 1970, regularly pulling in audiences of over fifteen million viewers.

After such a long and busy period in the sitting-rooms of the nation, Thora returned to the big screen with a leading role in the gloriously black comedy, *Some Will, Some Won't*, a remake of the 1951 Alastair Sim classic, *Laughter in Paradise*. Thora played a foul-tempered and arrogant woman who must serve as a lowly and down-trodden servant to gain her inheritance from an apparently deceased, eccentric rich uncle. Frank Thornton and Harold Goodwin provided useful support for Thora's harridan figure in the role originally played by Fay Compton. A sharper contrast couldn't have been imaginable when Michael Winner offered Thora the plum role of the housekeeper in his 1971 ghost story, *The Nightcomers*, with Marlon Brando and Stephanie Beacham.

By now Thora was in her sixties – though she had no intention of slowing down. The year 1972 brought her the opportunity to travel to Australia and star at the Perth Festival. Scottie and Thora loved to travel and this was too good an opportunity to miss. She appeared in Walter Greenwood's

Saturday Night at the Crown, a play she had appeared in literally hundreds of times before. Indeed, she played the part of Ada Thorpe for the thousandth time in her career on the second night of the festival and when the final curtain came down, a huge cake bedecked with glowing candles was wheeled on stage. Thora's trip to Australia was a huge success, partly ensured by her hit TV shows, *Meet the Wife* and *The First Lady*, being broadcast on Australian television to large audiences just weeks before her arrival.

Thora enjoyed her return to treading the boards and spent much of the next few years playing theatres across England. In 1976 the first part of her biography, *Scene and Hird*, was published.

In April 1977 Thora was back on the box in a one-off *Comedy Special*, *The Boys and Mrs B*, written by *Meet the Wife* creators Ronald Wolfe and Ronald Chesney. With Richard Caldicott, Gorden Kaye and the young Michael Deeks as the mischievous Dodger, Thora starred as the eponymous Mrs B, a local councillor who tries to control the members of a youth club with hilarious results. The production was in the more-than-capable hands of former *Hancock's Half Hour* producer Dennis Main Wilson but, sadly, no series resulted. A series did emerge from a 1969 pilot of *In Loving Memory* but not for ten years. In 1979 the first series was finally filmed and broadcast, even though Thora hadn't appeared in the original pilot production. She was cast as the no-nonsense funeral director Ivy Unsworth with her much-put-upon nephew, Billy Henshaw, played with relish by Christopher Beeny. Written by Dick Sharples and produced by Ronnie Baxter, the gentle, northern humour continued through five series up until 1986, by which time *In Loving Memory* had notched up an impressive twenty-nine weeks in the TV top twenty charts.

By that stage too, Thora had became the face of religious broadcasting, having started her seventeen-year presentation of the BBC's *Praise Be!* back in 1977. So it was a touch ironic that in the middle of that long run in the 'God slot' – as it became affectionately known – Dick Sharples returned to writing for Thora in two series of *Hallelujah!* This time Thora played Captain Emily Ridley, a no-nonsense, northern Salvation Army campaigner. Patsy Rowlands lent support through the 1983 and 1984 broadcasts and production was, once again, handled by Ronnie Baxter.

By now a respected and invaluable sitcom favourite, Thora was hardly given a chance to catch her breath once *In Loving Memory* had finished before the producer of her favourite show, *Last of the Summer Wine*, came a-calling. Having pioneered the notion of feature-length episodes on television, Alan J. W. Bell was fashioning a special edition of *Summer Wine* to introduce a new character – Seymour Utterthwaite as played by Michael Aldridge – following the departure of Brian Wilde as Foggy. Thora was invited to play the role of Seymour's sister, Edie Pegden, in the episode eventually screened as 'Uncle of the Bride', which gained a staggering eighteen million viewers during transmission on New Year's Day 1986. Billed as giving a 'special guest appearance', Thora has remained in the show ever since and is still credited as a guest among the regulars.

With regular work in the Yorkshire dales, Thora was also hotly pursued for other assignments. She made her last film appearance to date in the black chocolate comedy, *Consuming Passions* in 1988, as the overly fussy landlady of Tyler Butterworth. However, on television, Thora was to be awarded with some priceless pieces from Alan Bennett, including *Me! I'm Afraid of Virginia Woolf* in 1978 and two celebrated *Talking Heads* monologues, 'Cream Cracker Under the Settee' in 1988 and 'Waiting for the Telegram' a decade later, the latter two both winning her the much-coveted British Academy Award for Best Actress.

Still there was to be no sign of slowing down. Even though Thora was by now in her eighties, offers of work continued to roll in and, as well as still presenting *Praise Be!*, she found time to appear in prestigious dramas such as *Memento Mori* and episodes of long-running series, including *All Creatures Great and Small*, *Perfect Scoundrels* and *Heartbeat*.

Thora became Dame Thora Hird in 1993, and she received further recognition of her contribution to the entertainment world when she was presented with a Lifetime Achievement Award from BAFTA in the autumn of 1994. It was the industry's way of saying thank you and congratulations. For Thora, her career has always been about being lucky to be paid to do a job she loves. Yet Thora's love for acting has always taken second place to her love of her family. So Thora's life was shattered when her husband of over fifty years, Scottie, passed away just a few weeks later, following a stroke on 30 October 1994. He was eighty-eight. Unlike most widows, Thora decided the only thing to do to help with the pain was to continue working. Never happier than when on a stage or in a television studio, feeling the love of an adoring public was going to be her salvation.

And so she has continued. Long-time fan Victoria Wood tapped into Thora's iconography talents, offering her a role in the feature-length comedy drama *Pat and Margaret* – Thora was excellent as the fussy mother of Duncan Preston – and a supporting role in a single episode of *Dinnerladies*. Victoria also wrote a special two-hander for Thora and herself for the BBC's millennium celebration programme.

Summer Wine continued production towards and now beyond its two-hundredth episode, making it the world's longest-running television comedy series. Though no longer presenting *Praise Be!* Thora has continued making her annual pilgrimage to the Yorkshire dales, refusing to allow five hip operations and increasing immobility to prevent her from filming her treasured role of Edie Pegden.

And then in 1998, *Summer Wine* director Alan J. W. Bell moved from gentle comedy to tear-jerking drama as Thora took on the lead as Annie Longden in the television drama *Lost for Words*. Her role – as an aged mother suffering a series of strokes and the ensuing tribulations of being cared for by her ever-helpless yet so-patient son, played by Pete Postlethwaite – ensured that just a year after winning the BAFTA for Alan Bennett's 'Waiting for the Telegram', Dame Thora Hird became the oldest recipient of – as well as the first woman of the new millennium to win – the Best Actress Award at the grand age of eighty-nine.

Dame Thora Hird's career has lasted almost as long as the twentieth century itself. Starting on stage at eight weeks old and still working at ninety is an achievement few people can ever hope to equal. But Thora is loved by a nation not just because of the joy she has brought as an actress to generations of theatregoers and film and television viewers, but because everyone feels they know her. She's not Thora Hird OBE, Dame of the British Empire; she is someone who reminds us of Mum, Aunt or Granny. Thora continues to take pride of place in the heart of a whole nation; from the actors she has always unselfishly performed with to the charities she has worked quietly and tirelessly for over so many years, from the Prime Ministers she has reduced to fits of laughter to the everyday man and woman in the street who still, to this day, feel warmed by her presence. She is, quite simply, Our Thora!

Morris Bright

CHAPTER 1

Film & Theatre

The Black Sheep of Whitehall (1941)

It may have been sixty years ago, but I remember it as though it was yesterday. I was appearing in rep at the Royalty Theatre in Morecambe. That particular week the play was *As You Are*, and I was playing Emma Pearson, the sixty-year-old mother-in-law. I was only thirty, so on came the paste nose and heavy make-up.

As the curtain prepared to rise for the show, I could hear whispers that George Formby was in the audience. There was great excitement. He was a big name. After the show the manager brought him to meet me – apparently at George's personal request. I had no time to get all the make-up off before he turned up, so there I was with my paste nose all wonky, looking like I'd been in a fight. He said he was considering making a film version of *As You Are* and wanted me to come to Ealing Studios to
• audition for a part. I was dumbstruck.

So off to London I went, having borrowed from my aunts two fox furs that clipped together, and made me look rather grand, if overdressed. The moment I arrived at the studio gates, the air-raid sirens went off. Everyone started running and so I followed them. I ended up in a bomb shelter next to a woman who was shelling peas for the restaurant.

Finally the all-clear was given and off I went to be made up for the screen test. I was to test for the part of Lydia – the daughter-in-law of the character I played on stage. A young actor by the name of Bill Fraser had to call out the lines that George Formby would take in the film: 'Where will you go, Lydia?'

My reply was to be: 'I shall go to London' and then exit – hardly a measure of anyone's acting ability.

Anyway, we filmed this sequence ten

SIR JOHN MILLS

I am delighted to have this opportunity of being asked to recount my memories of working with dear Thora and well remember our appearances together in the film *The Long Memory* back in the early 1950s. A decade earlier we had both appeared in the very funny Will Hay comedy film, *The Black Sheep of Whitehall*, made at Ealing Studios. Always the consummate professional, Thora was always the envy of the rest of the cast as she never seemed to fluff any of her lines and indeed often used to act as a 'prompt' for everyone else.

I have followed her seemingly endless career over the years, both in films and on television, and would love to know the secret of what keeps her going. Her role in *Last of the Summer Wine* is a delight and long may she continue to bring joy to our screens during the years ahead.

times before I began to lose my cool. I thought, if I wasn't good enough by then, I never would be. And so on the eleventh take, I replied: 'I shall go to London and bugger you because I really don't think I'm very good at this and if I haven't done it right by now, I never will!' I heard a voice shout 'Cut!' I didn't know what that meant.

A rare shot of Thora, in a scene cut from the final print of *The Black Sheep of Whitehall*, in 1941.

Thora Hird appears in her first film, *The Black Sheep of Whitehall*, alongside comedy star, Will Hay. The film centres around an incompetent teacher mistaken for an economics expert who has been kidnapped by wartime spies. Thora appears for just three minutes at the beginning of the film, as Hay's poorly paid secretary.

The following morning I was told to go to the Rushes Theatre. I didn't know what that meant either. They sat me down in the viewing theatre to watch the shots from the previous day's filming. The room was full of people. When we got to my outburst, there was quite a bit of laughing, though I was speechless. The lights came back on and I was asked to report to the heads of the studios, Messrs Michael and Shandos Balcon. I felt like a schoolchild being sent to the headmaster's office.

The Balcons couldn't have been nicer. They told me I hadn't got the part of George Formby's mother because I looked too young, even with make-up. I remember thinking that at least I had my return train ticket home. And then

they came out with it. They wanted to offer me a seven-year contract with Ealing Studios, paying me ten pounds a day if I worked and ten pounds a week if I didn't. I told them that I couldn't take money for not working, that it wouldn't be right. Michael smiled, put his hands on my shoulders and wryly said: 'Don't ever say that again, Thora. You will do very well in this business, I am sure, and I have no doubt that one day you will be in this office complaining to me that we are not paying you enough.'

I returned home happy, and soon afterwards was back at the studios filming my part as the secretary in the Will Hay comedy, *The Black Sheep of Whitehall*. Over a dozen actresses had tested for the part and though Will wasn't keen on a newcomer taking the role, I got it nonetheless. I was on screen for all of three minutes, but it was the start of almost a quarter of a century of non-stop film parts for me.

Went the Day Well? (1942)

I loved *Went the Day Well?* It was one of those films that was made as a bit of a flag-waver during the war – a production that helped keep the morale of the country up after three long years of battle. Little did we know at the time that there were still three years to go.

It was only my second film too and this time I was playing a dairy girl from the country called Ivy Dawking. So out went the northern accent I was so used to from weekly rep and in came a slightly upper-class twang.

The plot centred around a group of villagers who tried to resist an invasion by German paratroopers. Of course we discover afterwards that the squire is a quisling, the swine. Anyway, we had to use rifles during filming and all the women insisted on firing the real thing. Boy, did they let off a huge bang! And if that wasn't bad enough, they pushed back as they fired and left me with a huge bruise on my shoulder. Still, it gave us an idea of what our men and boys were really going through out there on the front line, defending our country.

I had been needed for only two days' filming for *The Black Sheep of Whitehall*, but I was on set much longer this time round and it gave me a chance to meet a wonderful cast of actors and actresses, many of whom had been my heroes. Among them were Leslie Banks, Elizabeth Allen, Basil Sydney and Mervyn Johns.

My favourite actress in the film is still my favourite person to this day … my daughter Janette. She wasn't supposed to be in the film at all. She was barely four years old. But the director, Alberto Cavalcanti, was having a difficult time with a child actor who just couldn't get the part right. In typical Brazilian style, the director was getting flustered. Then he remembered he had seen Jan, when my husband Scottie had dropped me off at Ealing Studios that morning. It was a lovely day and the two of them went out to play on Ealing Common. Cavalcanti sent out two of his crew to search for them. I wouldn't give permission to film her until Scottie had said he was happy too. And that's how Jan got into show business and we made our first film appearance together.

Thora teams up with Elizabeth Allen to protect their village from invading Germans in the wartime melodrama *Went the Day Well?* The film was made and released in England in 1942, but it wasn't shown in the USA until 1944, where it was released under the title *48 Hours*.

One Good Turn (1954)

Thora and Norman Wisdom share a special comic moment in One Good Turn in 1954. It was Norman's second film of his seven-year contract for Rank – his first, Trouble in Store, having won him the British Academy Award for Best Newcomer in 1953.

You know, in this business there are some people who only have to look at you and you laugh. They have this ability not to move or say a thing and they are just hysterically funny. Tommy Cooper was one, but one of my favourites has always been Norman Wisdom. He is such a physical comedian and I used to think he made all his falls look so easy. But anyone in the business will tell you how hard Norman must have worked to get those movements just right.

We worked once together on film back in 1954, in *One Good Turn*. As always, I was playing a cook and Norman was helping out in an orphanage. We had some very funny business to do together, particularly a scene in a railway carriage where a wasp sets upon Norman, and a scene in the kitchen where we are peeling onions and both of us start out crying but end up in hysterics. If you watch the film you would think we weren't acting. Well, I can tell you we weren't. We really were laughing. Norman just set me off and we went on for ages. We had to re-shoot a couple of times and though the director John Paddy Carstairs started off by looking a little angry, by the end of it he too was in hysterics. It was one of the funniest days' filming of my entire career.

At the time Norman and I were both trying to give up smoking. I was being very good, but Norman had been seen having a swift drag between scenes. I went to props and asked them to make me up a huge chocolate box and then tipped the cleaners to gather together all the cigarette butts they could find from the studio floor that day. I packed them into this chocolate box, tied it with ribbon and had it sent to the London Palladium where Norman was appearing in the evenings. He came on boasting the next morning of his present, which he assumed was from an adoring fan. It wasn't until he opened it the next day, saw the contents and read the message – which I won't repeat here – that he realised he had been rumbled. But even then we shared a laugh. And we have done every time I have seen him since.

SIR NORMAN WISDOM

My first film, *Trouble in Stores*, had been a huge success in 1953. Straightaway Rank went into production with my second, called *One Good Turn*. In the film I was to play a handyman in an orphanage at which I had stayed on to live after growing up there myself. The orphanage is under threat from developers and I, along with the children, fight to keep it open.

The story was a special one to me. While I had never technically been an orphan myself, my own difficult childhood had often made me feel like I was. So among the humour there was much poignancy.

I was delighted to be working on that film with Thora Hird. By the time we made *One Good Turn*, Thora was already a well-established character actress in films. Thora played the cook and we spent all our time together trying not to giggle. We both have the sort of faces that the more you try and be serious the more you want to laugh.

Thora and I were both trying to stop smoking at the time and I promised to give up if she did. We both did quite well except I was spotted having a crafty one and Thora never let me forget it. I'll let her tell you that story.

We had some happy moments both on and off the set, from just larking about to judging a beauty contest ably assisted by Donald Sinden – who was also a huge Rank star of the 1950s. I was delighted to meet up with them both over forty years later when a plaque was unveiled in my name in the Hall of Fame at Pinewood Studios. I reminded Thora of the happy times we had shared together. And she reminded me of that sneaky cigarette.

What a great lady!

Thora returns to Pinewood Studios in 1997 to join in a special tribute celebrating Norman Wisdom's fifty years in show business. A plaque was unveiled in his honour by The British Comedy Society at the studios. Joining Norman and Thora are comedian Tom O'Connor and actor Sir Donald Sinden.

The Love Match (1955)

By the time the film version of *The Love Match* was to be made, I had already been appearing in the stage show on and off for two years. The play was written by Glen Melvyn, who was such a nice man. He had asked me to appear for some time, but I'd been busy. As soon as I became available I grabbed at it – first for a week at Wimbledon, then a short tour, then on to Brighton and a successful season in Blackpool. Finally the show arrived at the Palace Theatre, Cambridge Circus, where we played twice nightly. So by the time we got round to making the film, I sort of knew the part!

Arthur Askey and Thora Hird appear as Mr and Mrs Brown in Glen Melvyn's footballing farce, *The Love Match*. On stage the part of their daughter was played by Arthur's real life offspring, Anthea Askey. In the film version, the role was taken by actress and latterly Bond girl, Shirley Eaton.

That wonderful comic actor Arthur Askey and I played a husband and wife almost divided by his love for football. Now Arthur was a great performer, but on stage he did have a habit of trying to upstage his co-stars. My father always taught me that if you are upstaged once, than allow it. Twice, be wary. Three times, move down the stage.

One night I was doing a bit of business telling him that our son had scored for some team or another. I was wearing a veil on my hat, which was covered in large felt rings. As I spoke, the veil got caught in my mouth. It always got a laugh. But that night Arthur moved downstage about a yard, so I had to turn towards him and my face was obscured for half the audience. The laugh was smaller. The next night he moved further downstage and my laugh disappeared almost completely. In the second house that day I moved right to the front of the stage – nearly in the footlights. He couldn't move any further and the audience could see me. I got my laugh back. As we left the stage, he said, 'My, there's not a lot anyone can teach you about comedy, is there?' He never did it again after that.

SHIRLEY EATON

I did enjoy making *The Love Match*. It was such a funny film. But then, how could it not have been with such a cast of professionals? The film was only my second and I was just seventeen. I had made my first film – a cameo really – opposite Dirk Bogarde in *Doctor in the House* in 1953. In *The Love Match* I played the daughter to Thora and Arthur Askey and much of the plot surrounded me and my boyfriend, so the part was quite big.

Thora was very helpful and kind. She could see I was nervous and she was so encouraging. I remember that the part required a northern accent. Funnily enough I had been evacuated to Middleton near Manchester during the war and had picked up a bit of an accent then. When filming began and with a little help from Thora, it soon came back to me.

I enjoyed watching Thora and Arthur working together; they were a couple of old pros and of course had already appeared in *The Love Match* on stage. The daughter then was played by Arthur's own child, Anthea. So I was very lucky that they chose me to play the daughter in the film. It was ten years before I did *Goldfinger* and perhaps you could best describe me in those young days as pretty rather than sexy.

I next worked with Thora in *Sailor Beware* a few years later. Peggy Mount played my bombastic mother trying to put off my prospective sailor husband. Thora played the next-door neighbour who was always trying to poke her nose in. You know the sort I mean.

And though I haven't worked with her since then, I know I am one of millions who have been a fan of hers almost forever. Thora is a wonderful actress, but more importantly, she is such a wonderful person too.

Simon and Laura (1955)

Now here's a funny thing. As an actress you get used to playing all sorts of parts and having to be very adaptable. But at the end of the day, you are just acting, whether it is on stage, or film, radio or television. So imagine then that I get offered a part – yes, you've guessed it, as a cook – in a film in which I am filmed

MAURICE DENHAM

I am in my nineties now so I'll be honest and tell you that I can't remember a great deal about the film *Simon and Laura*. What I do remember – quite vividly – is sitting off-set with Thora and listening to her wonderful flow of hilarious 'anecdotes'. Certainly funnier than anything in the film, I am sure.

I send much love to Thora and Janette.

for a television show. That sounds very confusing, doesn't it? I'll explain.

The film was *Simon and Laura* and was a comedy about a show-business couple, played by the handsome Peter Finch and beautiful Kay Kendall, who allow television cameras to come into their home and film a real-life soap opera based on their everyday lives. I played the cook and my dear old friend Maurice Denham played the butler. Of course, being domestics to the stars we have our own delusions of grandeur and when we hear about the filming we

insist on playing ourselves in the programme. Before you say anything, it was a comedy. It was originally a hilarious stage farce, which played to huge crowds in the West End. Film versions of stage plays don't always work very well, but this one seemed to and it still makes me laugh to this day. But at the time, you can see how odd it must have been to stand in front of a film camera acting a part and then be asked for the character you are acting to act as another person. By the end of the day I couldn't work out who I was supposed to be.

If the face fits … Thora as a domestic to the stars in the 1955 all-star comedy *Simon and Laura*. Ian Carmichael (right) plays the young producer of a TV show to be shot at the house where Thora cooks and cleans.

Some Will, Some Won't (1969)

I've worked with some wonderful people over the years and have appeared in casts which read like an A to Z of British entertainment. I mean, look at *Last of the Summer Wine*, what a fine group of really professional actors and actresses and with that much acting experience behind them, it's staggering. And of course with *Summer Wine*, you can imagine that we spend so much time laughing while we are making the programme. It's a happy show, you see.

One of the funniest times I had working on a film was for the comedy *Some Will, Some Won't*, over thirty years ago now. It was the first film I had made in five years, having been rather busy on television with my shows, *Meet the Wife* and *The First Lady*. The film was about a rather snobbish family who had to undertake all manner of ridiculous and demeaning tasks to qualify for money left to them in the will of an eccentric rich uncle. I was probably the biggest snob of them all and when I had to pretend to be a hotel maid ... Well, can you imagine, *moi*? The results were hilarious. The cast, though, was even funnier. Just read these names and you'll know what it must have been like filming: Ronnie Corbett, Michael Hordern, Leslie Phillips, Arthur Lowe, Wilfrid

Thora and actor Frank Thornton, who played the frustrated and impatient hotel manager in the film comedy, *Some Will, Some Won't*. It was to be thirty years before the two got to work together again – albeit briefly – in *Last of the Summer Wine*.

FRANK THORNTON

At a casting conference in the offices of Linnit and Dunfee in 1954, the great farceur Ralph Lynn said of an actor whose name came up: 'Oh no, not him. He tries to be funny. You mustn't *try* to be funny. I don't try to be funny – (pause) – but, by God, I am funny.' One must remember, you see, that the character doesn't think he or she is funny; that is for the audience to decide.

Thora is a true exponent of the way to play comedy. She presents us with a real person whose existence we can believe in, someone who takes herself seriously and is thus quite oblivious to how funny she is.

In 1969 in the film *Some Will, Some Won't*, Thora was one of a family, all of whom had to perform an unpleasant or humiliating task in order to qualify for an inheritance. She played a bossy, snobbish lady who was required to get herself a job as a hotel chambermaid. I was the hotel manager who interviewed her for the job. Needless to say, she didn't get it.

So far, in my four years with *Last of the Summer Wine*, the nearest Truly has got to sharing a scene with Edie is one short but uncomfortable ride in the back of her little red Triumph Herald. We have never exchanged words and perhaps, with Truly dedicated to a pint in the pub and Edie dedicated to her coffee mornings, we never shall.

What a pity!

Brambell and lots more. And there was the man whose comedy work I've always admired over the years and who I see now flitting from pub to pub – for purely acting purposes, you'll understand – in his role in *Summer Wine*, Frank Thornton. He played the hotel manager in *Some Will, Some Won't* and gave me quite a ticking-off. It's all right though, it's taken me thirty years but I can get my own back on him now. Edie Pegden certainly wouldn't take any of that nonsense!

Ronnie Corbett, Leslie Phillips, Thora Hird and Michael Hordern look on expectantly as they wait to hear what tasks they must perform in order to inherit vast sums of money from their rich uncle's will in *Some Will, Some Won't*, the remake of the 1951 classic, *Laughter in Paradise*, which starred Alastair Sim and Joyce Grenfell.

RONNIE CORBETT OBE

I did enjoy *Some Will, Some Won't*. It was such a laugh. And I think it's probably the only time that I actually worked with Thora Hird. We didn't have too many scenes together once the film got underway – mainly in the early scenes when the 'family' convenes to hear what ridiculous tasks we are to undertake to get our hands on our dotty uncle's money. We did get the chance to sit and have a chat off-set, when Thora would be telling another wonderful story from her variety days while she had a quick cigarette. She'd talk of working with Freddie Frinton, not just on television but on stage and their special style of comedy, which I witnessed myself when I saw them both at the Palladium.

Thora really is a remarkable person. Her skills are so varied – from comedy to serious plays, there is nothing she hasn't been able to do. And with her variety background it is so uplifting to see her perform in award-winning drama, because in comedy it's so easy to get pigeonholed. Thora hasn't. And more power to her for that. She's so very resilient, an absolute delight and an example to us all.

A Kind of Loving (1962)

There are times in everyone's life when you know that something has happened that will make a real difference to your future. That applies to actors too, you know, normally with a part or a role that can have an impact on your career – good or bad, I suppose. I made a film, almost forty years ago now, which made a huge difference to my career. It was called *A Kind of Loving*, about a draughtsman who makes my virgin daughter pregnant and marries her against his will, and mine for that matter. He comes to live in my house and we hate each other from the start. That great actor and dear friend Alan Bates played the reluctant son-in-law and June Ritchie my daughter.

Alan Bates and Thora Hird off-set waiting for the next scene to be shot at a railway station during the making of *A Kind of Loving*.

The reason why the role was so important is that it gave me the chance to play a really dramatic lead role and show that I could do more than just play dotty chars or eccentric landladies on film. I had cut my acting teeth in serious roles on stage, but somehow never got the chance to do the same in front of a camera. Don't get me wrong, I've always loved comedy and anyone will tell you that playing comedy is often harder than serious drama, but I just wanted a chance to show what I could do. Thanks to the director John Schlesinger I got the chance.

I remember we were filming the infamous scene where Alan, blind drunk, comes in to my house late at night and proceeds, after a blazing row, to throw up on my carpet. In the script, I called him a pig. But John took me to one side and told me to imagine how I would feel with this drunken wretch who had impregnated my sweet innocent daughter, now defiling my home. 'Just let out anything that comes

---

JOHN SCHLESINGER,
Director of *A Kind of Loving*, speaking in 1996

I'm thinking back to 1962 and my first film, *A Kind of Loving*, where Thora played most brilliantly the monstrous mother-in-law to Alan Bates.

I remember the first day of shooting. I turned up on the set at the location in a car with Alan. I saw all the trucks, lighting and paraphernalia, and a large crew ... and, quite frankly, I was terrified. I wanted to turn round and run away. But there was Thora, at a window, waving a greeting and all ready to do the first scene.

She was not only wonderful in the scene but also tremendously encouraging to me personally. I was so tremendously uncertain and new at the game. She kept saying: 'It's going to be all right, love.'

A memorable scene that I will never forget was the now famous one where Alan Bates arrives home late at night, drunk, and Thora calls him a 'filthy dirty pig'.

I'll never forget working with her ... it was a tremendous experience.

to mind,' he said, 'within reason.' As the cameras rolled I thought of how I would have felt and the anger built up and out it came: 'You filthy pig, you filthy dirty pig!' But it wasn't just the words that came out, the sheer hatred of this woman for this horrible man came out as well.

John was very pleased and Alan didn't take it personally! We still get on famously well after all these years.

Life is anything but sweet for Vic Brown (Alan Bates) as tempers reach boiling point in the Rothwell household. Ingrid (June Ritchie) seems oblivious to the rantings of her mother (Thora Hird) in *A Kind of Loving*, 1962.

ALAN BATES

Thora had a grasp of her character immediately. She didn't have to work herself into a state to get it right. She has a huge trust in her own ability and quite rightly so. She is a naturally funny woman whose comedy is on the edge of tragedy. It's instinctive and very understanding of life itself.

She liked working with John Schlesinger and she loved the story of *A Kind of Loving*. She understood the suburban snobbishness of her character and no one could have played it better. Everyone talks about the scene where I am sick on her carpet and she calls me a filthy pig but the scene I remember most is one that we did together in a hospital where I have come to see my wife who has just suffered a miscarriage. That scene demanded Thora's character Mrs Rothwell to be at her most indulgent and self-righteous. Of course, the more self-righteous Thora acted it, the more I began to laugh, which set her off. We were both in hysterics and John had to hold up filming for almost an hour.

Thora is a one-off comedienne and a great actress.

KATHY STAFF

People imagine that I met Thora for the first time only when she joined the cast of *Last of the Summer Wine* in the 1980s. But we actually worked together forty years ago in *A Kind of Loving*. It was a dream come true for me, because Thora had always been my heroine as I grew up wanting to be an actress. Thora is one of the best actresses we have ever had in this country. In the film, I was cast as her next-door neighbour, Mrs Oliphant. I had two young daughters who they wanted to use in the film as extras, to play in the front garden. When we got to the location in Bolton the garden wasn't big enough for two children, so only one was required. I was in a panic as to what to do with my youngest, Susan.

Now, the scene was Alan Bates coming back to the house of his mother-in-law to find that his pregnant wife had fallen down the stairs and been rushed off to hospital. He hadn't been given a key by his dreadful mother-in-law, played by Thora, so I had to tell him that his wife was poorly.

My older daughter Katherine was riding round the garden on a bicycle while Susan, who was only two at the time, was being looked after inside the house by Thora. Today, Susan is a vicar. I often say to Thora, 'I wonder if it was thanks to your influence when you looked after her that day all those years ago.' It was a privilege to work with Thora then, and it has been again to work together all these years later on *Summer Wine*.

The Weaker Sex (1948)

I first appeared in the West End at the Vaudeville Theatre near the end of the war. I was starring in the play *No Medals* with Fay Compton and Frederick Leicester. It was a suburban comedy about the problems suffered by a war widow and I played – you guessed it – a cockney charlady of about sixty. The show ran for over two years and while it was a delight to have such regular work during wartime and, of course, to help bring some laughter to our war-torn capital, it wasn't an easy time for me personally. You see, Scottie was away in the Air Force and our daughter Janette – who was only four – had been evacuated to Lancashire, being looked after by our nanny Vera. And I don't like my own company really, so things were a bit lonely. I made lots of friends, though, during the run and we did share lots of laughs. One night I was leaving the

theatre and there was a rather large dog standing by the billboard outside, appearing to read the cast list. It lifted its leg and peed all over my name, which was quite a job I can tell you as it was in the smallest of print at the bottom of the poster. My first West End play and what a review!

The show was so popular that they made it into a film in 1948 with a great cast that included Cecil Parker, Lana Morris, and someone I was to work with again over forty years later in *Last of the Summer Wine* – my late and much-missed friend, Bill Owen. Many people who watch *Summer Wine* assume that is all that Bill was ever known for. He started playing the part of Compo aged fifty-seven. But in fact like so many others of us in the cast, he'd had a long career dating back the best part of half a century. It's odd looking back, thinking of someone you worked with in the late 1940s and whom you were working with again in the late 1990s. I was with Bill on set on the last days he filmed for *Summer Wine*. He was such a professional, acting through the pain of his cancer. A real trouper and a lesson to us all. I remember him with great affection.

A publicity shot from the 1948 wartime comedy, *The Weaker Sex*, showing charlady Mrs Gaye (Thora Hird) and Geoffrey Radcliffe (Cecil Parker) doing a little product placement for Hoover!

Once a Jolly Swagman (1948)

Things went a bit quiet on the acting front for a while in 1948. I had made a few films early on that year but my Ealing contract was coming to an end and there was little on offer in the way of stage work. Then I was asked to go and see a director called Frederick Piffard at the New Lindsey Theatre in Notting Hill. He was putting on a play called *Flowers for the Living*. I was given a script and started to rehearse the part of Shirley for an imminent audition. But Shirley was supposed to be the fifteen-year-old cockney daughter of a Mr and Mrs Holmes, and by then I was already thirty-seven! I've always tried to keep young-looking but that was ridiculous. When the director called me I told him I thought I was totally unsuitable for the role of Shirley. 'I agree', he said, 'I want you to play Mrs Holmes, the mother.' One half of me was relieved, the other a little disappointed, particularly when I read the description of the character: 'a shabby, hard-worked, middle-aged cockney woman, who looks like she's going through the change'! I got the part.

It seemed to be the beginning of a very special time for me. I got a seven-year contract with Rank and the film parts started rolling in. One of my favourites was *Once a Jolly Swagman* in which I had to play the mother of a speedway rider, Bill Fox. Bill was played by Dirk Bogarde, who was a delight to work with. He had such good looks, charm and he was a good actor too. Now there's something you don't see every day. And you wouldn't have believed it was only his second film, he was that professional. I did enjoy playing Dirk's mother, even though I was only ten years older than he was. All make-up, of course.

A young Dirk Bogarde stars as Bill Fox in the 1948 melodrama, *Once a Jolly Swagman*. Thora appeared as Bill's mother.

The Nightcomers (1971)

Director Michael Winner sets up Oscar-winning international star Marlon Brando for his next scene in the 1971 film, *The Nightcomers*. Thora Hird, who can be seen in the background, played the bossy governess, Mrs Gross.

Now, I'm not one for swanking because you already know that over the years I've worked with some pretty big names on stage and film and television. But I am sure you can imagine the surprise I got when I was approached to star opposite Marlon Brando in the film *The Nightcomers*. It was in the early 1970s and by then I had reached sixty – not really the best time to meet such a handsome, big international film star, I suppose. Marlon would have been in his mid-forties by then and he was certainly a presence to be reckoned with. I don't mean that in a bad way. He was a big star and he knew that, but there was no arrogance or stand-offishness, certainly not to me at least. Michael Winner was the director of that film. He seemed very young indeed. But he appeared to know what he was doing, and I was impressed by the fact that he always liked to shoot on location rather than build sets in a studio somewhere. It certainly seemed to work for this film. Very eerie and odd it was, with murder and peculiar sexual exploits going on. I hadn't made a film for two years at that stage because I had been so busy with *The First Lady* on television, so it was an interesting if rather macabre return to the silver screen.

I didn't make another film for five years after that. I'm not blaming it on Michael or Marlon. Not at all. No, they were great to work with. It's just stage, television and a tour of Australia kept me away for a time. But I will always be proud to say that I got to work with Marlon Brando, particularly as the next year he won the Oscar for his role in *The Godfather*.

MICHAEL WINNER

I first met Thora Hird when I was fifteen years old, in 1950. I was working, while still at school, as a columnist on the *Kensington Post* group of newspapers. I interviewed her daughter Janette. I had tea with Thora and her husband and Janette in Bayswater near the park. We met a number of times thereafter and I was delighted to employ her in *The Nightcomers* because she is a fantastic actress.

The idea of Thora Hird working alongside Marlon Brando was quite amusing and they worked together very well. She played the bossy governess Mrs Gross, who was appalled at everything and everybody. Marlon played Peter Quint, the Irish gardener, up to no good in a prelude to the *Turn of the Screw*, with all the same characters in it.

The best you could say of Thora is that she is a consummate professional. She turns up, she knows her lines, she delivers them absolutely brilliantly and without any fuss. In between times she sits and talks about the industry and the things she is doing that are fascinating to her and interesting to other people. She is one of the great actresses and one of the great characters of British drama and I am very thrilled that we were at last able to make a movie together so many years after I first met her and her family.

The Cure for Love (1949)

Most people don't imagine that those of us who are in the industry actually have our own heroes among the actors and actresses we have had the chance to work with. But we do, you know. I was quite taken aback and rather touched when Nora Batty actress Kathy Staff from *Last of the Summer Wine* admitted to me that I was one of her biggest heroines and influences when she was growing up and starting in the business. That really is a compliment, especially when you see what a good and popular actress Kathy is.

Well, I've had my heroes too. One of them was the tall and suave actor Robert Donat who made some wonderful films in the 1930s and won an Oscar for his role in *Goodbye, Mr Chips*. So you can imagine how delighted I was to be cast in a film in which he was not just starring but actually directing, called *The Cure for Love*. The film was based on a play by another hero of mine, the writer Walter Greenwood. I appeared on stage many times over the years in Walter's plays and though we would argue and argue about a line he may have written for me, we became great friends. And he knew about working for success. His play, *Love on the Dole*, about life among unemployed Lancashire cotton workers – now regarded quite rightly as a classic – was returned to him thirty-nine times before it was published. Can you believe that?

Anyway, in the film, I was playing Mrs Doorbell, the aged woman who apparently knows the 'cure for love'. Back came the rubber make-up again to make me look old. Now, I was also appearing on stage in London at night and since there was no time to change after the day's shooting, I had to 'unpeel' myself in the car on the journey back into town each evening. Goodness only knows what the other drivers must have been thinking as we stopped at all those traffic lights.

Oldham Repertory (1955)

Any actor who started their career on the stage will tell you that there's nothing quite like working in front of a live audience. When they laugh in a comedy there's no feeling that can lift you higher. Even during those special moments when an audience is silent during the most dramatic of scenes, even that silence – or I suppose knowing that all those hundreds of people are being silent because of what you are saying or doing on stage – is so thrilling.

So I was delighted to return to my old stomping ground at Oldham Rep in the mid-1950s to appear in my friend Walter Greenwood's hilarious play *Saturday Night at the Crown*.

The play may have been funny but the billboard at the front of the theatre in Oldham took the biscuit. In large capital letters it read:

WORLD PREMIERE OF
WALTER GREENWOOD'S

SATURDAY NIGHT AT THE CROWN

STARRING THORA HIRD.

World Premiere in Oldham? Please don't misunderstand me. I am not trying to do Oldham down. I have always enjoyed working there, but I did think the words 'World Premiere' were over-egging it a little.

During the run, we would pop across to the Grapes pub, which had a smashing singing room where locals would stand up and belt it out every night. One evening before the show was about to finish, we all went in to be greeted by a man on stage singing 'Only a rose' – or the way he was singing it, 'Hone-lee a roez'. Suddenly the master of ceremonies got up, pushed the singer to one side and started speaking into the microphone: 'Ladies and gentlemen, there is somebody here tonight who has been gracing us with her presence on stage at the Coliseum [Oldham Rep] this past two weeks and whom we all love very much. I have to introduce you to her and I would like to call her up on stage to say hello and goodbye, since she's off home tomorrow. Yes, it gives me great pleasure to introduce you to … Janette Scott's mother!' After such a build-up too. And that's why I've never got big-headed in this business!

Thora takes a break from rehearsals for *Saturday Night at the Crown* at Oldham Rep, to share a cup of tea, a cigarette and a joke with cast members and friends, including actor Frank Middlemass (immediate right of Thora).

DAVID RUSTIDGE,
House Manager, Oldham Coliseum Theatre

Thora appeared in the Walter Greenwood comedy, *Saturday Night at the Crown* at the Oldham Coliseum in 1956. It was lucky for her because during the interval on the third night, she received a visit from one Kathleen Williams from Blackpool, who told her that her company had bought the play for the season. While in Oldham, Thora stayed at a local pub called The Grapes. During an after-show social night, the pub manager announced to a lively set of customers that they should not be too raucous as they were in the presence of Janette Scott's mother. Miss Scott was a popular film star at the time. Thora subsequently appeared in *Happy Days* in 1958 when she played the second act as a monologue with her stage husband soundly asleep in bed.

Blackpool (1953)

Thora (front right) studies the next contestant while she and Arthur Askey judge a seaside beauty contest during their season-long stage run of *The Love Match* at Blackpool in 1953.

Before making the film version of the comedy *The Love Match*, I toured with the show around the country before a sell-out season in the West End. Rather than just a week here and a week there we played a whole season at the Grand Theatre in Blackpool in 1953. It was my first introduction to that truly magnificent theatre and it was the start of a long friendship with both the Grand and its audiences.

Arthur Askey, who starred with me in *The Love Match*, enjoyed Blackpool too and we were regularly invited throughout the run to attend one event or another in the town. You know the sort of thing I mean – judging all sorts of competitions from the most beautiful babies to the most glamorous grannies, and most importantly the local beauty contests, which they seemed to hold every week or so as a new batch of holidaymakers came for a break at the seaside. It always amazed me how smartly people would dress just to sit in a deckchair on the beach. Always a jacket, sometimes a tie and normally a hat for the men and the women wore lovely dresses. You're lucky if people wear anything at all on our beaches today.

One incident, which happened when *The Love Match* moved to London, still makes me laugh to this day. Arthur and I were doing a bit of business and suddenly we heard this loud noise coming from the stalls. It sounded like someone shelling peanuts. We carried on for a while but it got too much for Arthur who walked to the front of the stage, leaned over and said: 'Pass us a couple while you're finishing them. We'll wait. You're louder than we are.' It got such a laugh.

The Entertainer (1960)

You always hear it in our business, don't you, that film versions of stage shows don't work as well because the words are written by a playwright to be performed in the intimacy of a theatre, and not meant to be given the big screen treatment where some of the feeling is lost? I don't always agree with that. I've appeared in several film versions of stage plays and I think that if you have a good writer and a good director, there's no reason why a film can't be just as believable as a play. Of course, if you have the right actors too, your job is complete.

That's what it felt like working on the film *The Entertainer* with the late Larry Olivier. He had been a great triumph in the stage version, playing the faded seaside comic Archie Rice, and the moment I saw him acting in front of the cameras, I knew he was going to be just as good. And he was. Larry was nominated for the Oscar for Best Actor that year.

We had a great cast for that film, which included Alan Bates – two years before he was sick on my carpet in *A Kind of Loving*; a young and very handsome Albert Finney; Larry's future wife Joan Plowright; and a wonderful young actress who played my daughter, Shirley Anne Field. She was a beauty. She still is for that matter. And my character did treat her badly in the film, trying to get her into show business at almost any cost!

For me, filming felt like being back home. Well, in fact, I was back home. Much of the exterior filming was done in and around the Morecambe area. Indeed the director used the outside of the Alhambra Theatre for several scenes – the very theatre which my dear Dad, God bless him, had stage-managed half a century earlier.

Thora's looking very pleased as daughter Shirley Anne Field tries to win over Laurence Olivier in the 1960 British classic, *The Entertainer*.

Further Up the Creek (1959)

Thora joins friend Frankie Howerd on set for the 1959 nautical romp, *Further Up the Creek*.

The sort of comedians I've always admired are those who can make you laugh at the bat of an eyelid, the sort who make it look so easy, but who really have to work so hard at it. My dear friend Frankie Howerd was like that. You'd imagine, wouldn't you, when you hear all those 'oohs' and 'aahs', that he was just saying them as and when he wanted. But I can tell you that Frankie rehearsed and rehearsed them to get his timing just right and turn what might sometimes have been just a little gag into a real belter. And

he had to overcome a stammer in early life that you'd never have known about if he hadn't told us all about it.

We appeared together in one film, a nautical comedy, *Further Up the Creek*, which was the sequel to *Up the Creek*, in which Frankie had also appeared the year before. We got on so well that he invited me to tour the pantomime circuit with him. I think I was a bit of a mother figure to him, you see, and he enjoyed my company. I went round to his house one day in Holland Park and sat with some of his theatrical friends.

He made tea for us all and they all had to drink it out of a mug, but I got the china cup.

We never did the panto season together. The producers wanted me to play dame and I said no. Well, you all know that a man has to play dame. That's what makes it so funny, isn't it?

I can't believe that it's been almost ten years since Frankie passed away. He was so funny, right up to the end. And it didn't surprise me to learn when he died, that he'd been fibbing about his age. He was seventy-five and not seventy, you know. Well, I can hardly lie about my age now, can I? This could hardly be a ninetieth birthday book about my life if I was only eighty-five!

Sailor Beware (1956)

The one thing you have to be careful about in our business is typecasting. You can play a part, or the same sort of part, so often that people think that's all you can do and that's all you get offered. And even if the casting directors and producers know that you can play something else, they're nervous to give you the part because viewers will either expect you to be a certain way or possibly be disappointed if you are not. You know what I mean. You see it with a lot of those people who star in soaps and regular weekly shows.

Thora joins two other stalwarts of British cinema, Esma Cannon and Peggy Mount (second and third left), playing the noisy neighbour in the 1956 marital farce Sailor Beware.

I've been very lucky, really. I did spend a lot of time in my early cinema days playing charladies and cleaners and so on, but I wasn't really known well enough to be typecast. People thought they'd seen me before but couldn't be sure. As I've said before, it could as easily have been one of the other actresses they used to cast in those sorts of roles, like Kathleen Harrison or Esma Cannon.

I appeared with Esma in *Sailor Beware*, which was a very funny film about a

sailor having trouble with his mother-in-law-to-be, played by Peggy Mount. Now if anyone was going to be at risk from typecasting it was Peggy. She played all those wonderful 'dragon'-like characters, frightening the life out of all the men – and women – around her. Peggy isn't like that, though. Not 'in real life', as we say. She's always been a real softy and one of the nicest and kindest people you could wish to meet, or work with for that matter. She did make me laugh in *Sailor Beware*, the way she treated the men. It reminded me of all those big, bossy, bosomy women that used to shop in the Co-op when I was a check-out girl in the 1920s. Gave me a few ideas how to play some of my roles over the years, I can tell you.

Turn the Key Softly (1953)

Veteran British actress Kathleen Harrison plays Mrs Quilliam, a newly released prisoner, appealing to the better nature of landlady Mrs Rowan as played by Thora Hird in the 1953 melodrama, *Turn the Key Softly*.

Turn the Key Softly was my thirtieth film in eleven years. You'd imagine that I would have graduated from my early bit parts as a maid or cleaner to something a little more grandiose. Well, you'd be wrong. Here I am again playing a landlady, Mrs Rowan I think her name was. I seem to remember the film being about a group of women who leave prison all on the same day and how they cope with being back out in the real world. One of the ladies was played by a very young and pretty Joan Collins. She turned a few heads, I can tell you. Mind you, she still does. In this picture, though, you can see my dear old friend Kathleen Harrison. This picture always brings a smile to my face. Not because the film was funny, you understand, far from it. It was a very serious drama indeed and I played a none-too-pleased and very unsympathetic landlady when Kathleen came knocking on my door for somewhere to live.

No, there used to be a bit of a joke within the industry in those days that if you were looking for someone for a day's shooting here or there to play a maid or a char, a landlady or cook, then call on Thora Hird. If she's busy, try Kathleen Harrison or Esma Cannon. Doris Hare, who went on to be so funny as the mother in *On the Buses*, was the fourth choice and occasionally Dora Bryan got in on the act, though she was a bit younger and tended to get the tarty barmaid parts – I know she'll forgive me for saying that. Very occasionally two or three of us would all appear in the same film. This was one and I remember appearing with Esma a few years later in the comedy, *Sailor Beware*.

CHAPTER 2

Changing Faces

Thora Hird 1911-2001

Thora aged 3, 1914.

Thora aged 7, 1918.

Thora aged 10, 1921.

Thora aged 16, 1927.

Thora aged 18, 1929.

Thora aged 35, 1946.

Thora aged 37, 1948.

Thora aged 38, 1949.

Thora aged 38, 1949.

Thora, early 1950s.

Thora aged 44, 1955.

Thora, early 1960s.

Thora aged 57, 1968.

Thora, early 1960s.

Thora, late 1960s.

...ora, early 1980s.

Thora aged 77, 1988.

...ora, early 1980s.

Thora aged 84, 1995.

Thora's 90th Birthday

28 May 2001

Thora salutes two Chelsea pensioners, Archie Harrington and 'Tug' Wilson, at the Lord Mayor's tea.

The icing on the cake – showbusiness friends join Thora to celebrate her 90... day. (Left to right: comedian Barry Cryer, producer/director Alan J. W. Be... Chris Beeny, agent Felix de Wolfe, actress Kathy Staff, and, in the front, d... Janette Scott.)

Thora takes tea with the Lord Mayor of Westminster, Harvey Marshall, while close acting friend, Frank Middlemass, looks on.

More greetings for the birthday girl!

Thora surrounded by family and friends for a celebration lunch at the Sloane Club.

CHAPTER 3

Television

Romeo and Juliet (1967, BBC)

I don't know if it was because I was still jet-lagged after a trip away to visit my daughter Jan and husband Mel Tormé in America for Christmas, but I actually turned down the part of Nurse in the BBC's 1967 version of *Romeo and Juliet*. They had been casting for their *Play of the Month* season and, not feeling too keen to follow the likes of Dame Edith Evans and Dame Flora Robson and not having ever really wanted to play the role, I just turned it down. Politely, of course.

What I didn't know was that the producer Cedric Messina and director Alan Cooke had almost set their hearts on me taking the role and weren't going to take my refusal without putting up a fight. I was asked again and then invited out to one of those lunches. You know the ones I mean. Plenty of food, wine, soft music and soft soap. Alan asked why I didn't want the role and I pointed out that Nurse is always played as an old woman, but she shouldn't be because she had wet nursed Juliet just fourteen years previously. 'Exactly', he said, flooring me a little. He explained that he wanted me to play Nurse younger and, because I was a woman of around

Thora appears as Nurse alongside a young Hywel Bennett in the 1967 BBC production of Shakespeare's Romeo and Juliet.

fifty, I would be ideal. Well, maybe it was the compliments, but the next morning I changed my mind and agreed to take the part. I have to admit that I was glad that I did. I thoroughly enjoyed getting my teeth into Shakespeare and hoped that wherever he was he forgave me, along with all the actresses before me, for making Nurse a bit younger than had been played over the years. Unfortunately I never got to see the finished drama when it was broadcast as I was busy putting the finishing touches to the first series of *The First Lady*.

The Queen Came By (1955, BBC)

It's hard to believe that I was born just seven years after Queen Victoria died. Why do I mention this to you? Well, one of my favourite roles was that of Emmie Slee in a stage play called *The Queen Came By*. The play was written by R. F. Delderfield, whose book *The Bull Boys* was the inspiration for that long-running series of film comedies, the *Carry On* films. But I digress. His play was set in a draper's shop in 1887, the year of Queen Victoria's golden jubilee.

I first played the part at the Embassy Theatre, Swiss Cottage and then the Duke of York's in the West End. I remember how proud I was when my little daughter Janette came to watch me one night, though she got a little upset at the end when Emmie was taken ill. She was too young to understand, you see. Some years later I was invited to play Emmie in a television version of the play and because dramas went out live in those days, with no tapes of the shows, the BBC decided to put it on again two years after that.

Well, imagine my surprise when Jan rang me up and told me that she would be playing the sixteen-year-old girl, Kitty Tape. By then Jan was a film star and the BBC had to get special permission from Associated British to let her appear. We shared top billing, of course.

It was the only time that Jan and I appeared in a play together and it was probably the happiest and proudest production I've ever been in because of that.

Mother and daughter appear on 'stage' for the only time in their careers as Thora and Janette Scott star in the 1957 BBC production of R. F. Delderfield's *The Queen Came By*.

Dixon of Dock Green (1966, BBC)

It's back to 'old before her time' parts as Thora appears in BBC television's long-running police drama series, *Dixon of Dock Green* in 1966.

Scottie always used to ask me why it was that I wouldn't take just a few minutes off from time to time. In the early days, when I was getting my career off the ground, I never wanted to stop in case the work stopped coming in, and I was happy to use what seemed like endless energy in those days appearing in films by day and on stage by night.

By the mid-1960s with Palladium seasons running almost at the same time as shows on television, I suppose Scottie had a point. *Meet the Wife* on the BBC was doing very well and so were the variety runs in between. But if I got offered a part that I fancied I still tried not to turn it down unless my schedules just wouldn't allow it. That's how I ended up in *Dixon of Dock Green* in 1966. The show had already been running for eleven years by then, and it was such a popular show that the whole country enjoyed – including me and Scottie – that I was happy to take on the role of a very aged woman. By then I was in my mid-fifties and I noticed it was taking less and less time to make me look old! Mind you, dear old Jack Warner was over seventy and still playing a police constable. Now that's what I call make-up.

Yes, 1966 was a busy year. I remember appearing in *Call My Bluff, The Good Old Days, Jackanory* and *Late Night Line Up*. I also did thirty-two weeks at the Palladium, had a short holiday in France and made an advert for Biotex!

Praise Be! (1977-93, BBC)

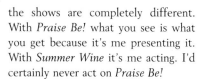

The face of religious broadcasting for a generation, a beaming Thora outside Broadcasting House in London, during her seventeen-year stint presenting *Praise Be!*

Seventeen years does seem a long time to be in one television programme, though I've almost managed that twice now. First there was *Praise Be!* which I presented from the late 1970s through the 1980s and into the 1990s, and now I'm coming up for seventeen years in *Last of the Summer Wine*. Of course, the shows are completely different. With *Praise Be!* what you see is what you get because it's me presenting it. With *Summer Wine* it's me acting. I'd certainly never act on *Praise Be!*

I've always been a religious woman, as you know, and while I'm not saying that presenting the programme made me more religious, it made me more aware of religion and people and their lives. Viewers wouldn't just write in because they wanted to hear a particular hymn, but because they needed someone to tell their troubles to. Many were elderly and recently widowed and their stories were heart-rending. Often was the night that Scottie would come into the bedroom to find me in floods of tears after reading another sad letter. He got so upset that he threatened to stop me doing the programme. But I never did. Not until they stopped making it.

It wasn't all difficult though. *Praise Be!* was a wonderfully uplifting programme to present. For every sad letter there would be a happy one and those that unintentionally made me laugh. If I tell you the number of letters that started 'Dear Dora' or 'Dear Nora' you wouldn't believe it.

Some people used to ask how I could present a religious programme while appearing at the same time in comedies such as *In Loving Memory* and *Hallelujah!* Well, these shows may have poked a bit of fun occasionally at 'religious types' but never at religion itself, and certainly never maliciously because, if they had, you know I would never have appeared in them.

In Loving Memory (1979-86, YORKSHIRE TELEVISION)

The first question I asked when I was presented with a script for *In Loving Memory* was, 'Could it ever hurt anybody that has been bereaved?'

The writer Dick Sharples said, 'Do you think we would have brought it to you if it could?'

That was enough for me. The script was very funny and I was keen on doing the show. I played Ivy Unsworth, the wife of an undertaker who dies in the first episode, leaving me to run the business with the help of my hapless nephew Billy, played so marvellously by Christopher Beeny.

The show ran for five series and yet anyone I speak to seems to remember only the very first episode where a coffin falls out of the hearse, shoots down a hill and ends up in a canal, with all the mourners having to throw the wreaths into the water like some burial at sea.

I did worry a lot about hurting people's feelings and upsetting anyone who may have been bereaved but the fan letters came flooding in for the show and so many people said how nice it was to be able to have a bit of a laugh over a subject which we can be so strait-laced about. And if you think about it, loving memories bring great joy and laughter, so why shouldn't *In Loving Memory*? One young lady wrote and told me how her uncle had wanted to be cremated but that his widow insisted he be buried. On the way to the cemetery the hearse had to stop because it had caught fire and they had to leave the coffin on the pavement while they got another vehicle. 'My uncle almost got his wish,' she joked.

Hearse today, gone tomorrow. Chris Beeny as Billy and Thora as Ivy Unsworth in Yorkshire Television's long-running undertakers comedy, *In Loving Memory*.

CHRIS BEENY

I was on holiday in Portugal when my agent phoned and asked me if I would like to record a pilot episode of a new series, *In Loving Memory*. When he told me it was with Thora Hird the decision was made. How could I possibly refuse the opportunity of working with one of our finest actresses? I first met Thora on the London-to-Leeds train and from the moment we met I knew we would get on. Thora has a unique knack of making people feel special. I became a close friend and one of her extended family and I am pleased to say that that has endured to this day.

Recording the series was great fun. I remember one particular occasion when we broke for lunch and, as Thora and I were across the other side of the valley in the hearse, the director suggested that I should drive us both to the restaurant. We therefore arrived, in full funereal regalia, ahead of the rest of the crew and parked outside. We had barely settled ourselves at our table when the maître d'hôtel, who was obviously unaware that the TV crew had booked the whole restaurant, approached our table and asked discreetly, 'Excuse me, Sir, Madam, would you mind moving your hearse? It's putting off our other customers.'

We recorded the studio scenes of *In Loving Memory* in Leeds on a Friday evening. Like me, Thora liked to get home, me to my wife and her to her beloved husband, Scottie. As soon as the recording finished we would race out of the studios and I would drive down the M1 to London. That's when I really got to know Thora and we would chat all the way home. I also found out one of her little secrets: she loves chocolate raisins and would munch them by the bagful.

Hallelujah! (1982-84, YORKSHIRE TELEVISION)

Dear old Dick Sharples, who wrote *In Loving Memory* for me, then wrote another series – at the same time – called *Hallelujah!* in which I was to play Salvation Army Captain Emily Ridley, who had forty-two years' service under her belt. Of course, the top brass want her to retire, but instead

The cast of *Hallelujah!* prepare for their new series. Patsy Rowlands (left) as Alice Meredith and Rosamund Greenwood (right) as Dorothy Smith with Thora as Captain Emily Ridley. The show ran for two series and fifteen episodes in the early 1980s.

of breaking the difficult news they banish her to a quiet town called Brighouse. Well, it would have been quiet if Emily hadn't been one for sniffing out sin even where none is lurking.

Again, I was a bit worried about offending viewers, particularly as I have always had a soft spot myself for the Sally Army – I have visited them on many occasions over the years and happily taken part in Bible readings. Naturally, I didn't want it to look as though I was having a laugh at their expense. So we got in a technical adviser from the Salvation Army to let us know if we were taking things a bit too far. According to the officer, we weren't taking things far enough!

One day we were filming out of doors, and I was wearing my tight-fitting Salvation Army uniform when the sound man came to fix me with my microphone to help pick up my voice on tape. He was having trouble finding somewhere to conceal it without anyone noticing it in shot. He hid the microphone on my blouse and clipped the receiver on to the back of my skirt. To hide the wires from one to the other he had to pass them up the inside of my skirt. So imagine the sight that greeted onlookers. There's me standing in the middle of a street with a man lying on the floor with his hand up my skirt. Two women walked past with their groceries and one muttered to the other: 'It's okay, it's only Thora he's doing it to, so that's all right!'

Highway WITH HARRY SECOMBE (CENTRAL TELEVISION)

Two great show business pals united by religion, as Thora joins Harry Secombe during the making of *Highway* in Morecambe Bay.

While I was presenting *Praise Be!* for the BBC, Harry Secombe was presenting ITV's Sunday late-afternoon religious programme, *Highway*. There was no serious competition between us because we were the best of friends. With around seven million viewers for each of our shows, it's not bad to be

pulling in all those people to watch religious programming, whoever may be presenting it.

Harry and I first worked together in the 1950s, long before a thirty-two-week run in *London Laughs* at the London Palladium in 1966. I remember that show very well. I appeared with my screen husband Freddie Frinton for some very funny sketches. Anita Harris was one of the wonderful singers, and there was a new comic on the block who had the audiences in stitches every night – Jimmy Tarbuck was his name. I remember that Harry and I opened the second half of the show as a cockney pearly king and queen riding onto the stage in a cart pulled by an exceptionally well-behaved donkey.

For years, Harry and I used to say how nice it would be if, one day, one of us could appear on the other's religious

SIR HARRY SECOMBE

I first worked with Thora at the Palladium in the late 1950s. She was and still is such a professional, and an incredibly funny lady indeed. Whenever we meet we always end up falling about laughing. She's so down to earth, you see. What you see with Thora is what you get. As with many people, in this business you may not see a friend for some time, but with Thora, you just pick up where you left off.

When I used to make *Highway* for ITV, Thora was making *Praise Be!* for the BBC. Whenever I was out filming on location, if I saw a camera crew go by, I would shout out: 'There goes Thora!'

She did actually appear on *Highway* with me, when we met up at Morecambe Bay. We had a wonderful day together and it was a unique privilege to have her on my show.

She's such a great lady and to win those BAFTAs for acting at her age just goes to show what a brilliant artiste she is too.

---

show. It finally happened in the 1980s when Harry and his team brought their travelling programme to film at my home town of Morecambe. When he invited me to appear on his show there, of all places, I could hardly turn him down. We had such a nice day together.

It was a delight and a privilege to appear with Harry. Like myself, he was a person of great faith, which I know helped him in his times of personal illness. And Harry was such an example to us all. He never complained but always managed to have a laugh and look on the bright side of life. I loved him very dearly and though he never made it on to *Praise Be!* with me, I was delighted to take part in a special *Songs of Praise* tribute to him, recorded in his presence and in his honour during 2000.

Intensive Care (1982, BBC)

Because I won the British Academy Award for Best Actress for 'Cream Cracker Under the Settee' in 1988 and again for 'Waiting for the Telegram' in 1998, most people seem to think – because of the attention they got, I suppose – that these were the only times I worked with that great writer, Alan Bennett. But that's not the case at all.

Alan's been writing for me – I don't mean as though I pay him as a writer, but writing parts with me in mind to play them – since 1978. I first appeared in one of his television works called *Me! I'm Afraid of Virginia Woolf*. In fact it was in that play that I had one of my funniest lines ever. My son Trevor is at the polytechnic – which I insisted on calling 'college' – when during a conversation he mentions the word 'lesbian'. Now you can tell by the look on my face that my character doesn't know what that means but isn't going to let on. Eventually, curiosity gets the better of her and she asks him what a lesbian is.

'Oh, mother. It's a woman who sleeps with another woman!'

There's a pause while I'm thinking, before I say quite nonchalantly: 'Well that's nothing! I slept with your Auntie Phyllis all during the air-raids!'

Hilarious stuff. But that's Alan for you. Just a couple of words and a look and he can have you laughing or crying as quickly as that.

I worked with Alan again in 1979 in *Afternoon Off*, before appearing as his mother in his play, *Intensive Care*, for BBC's *Play for Today* season in 1982. Well, the rest, as they say, is history, isn't it? He's continued to write some of my happiest work for me and I hope that before long we'll get the chance to work together again. I really do.

The First Lady (1968-70, BBC)

I used to say that there were two 'Alans' in my life – Alan Bennett who wrote those wonderful plays for me in the 1980s and 1990s, and before him Alan Plater who was responsible for my first big hit drama series on television, *The First Lady*, in the late 1960s.

The First Lady was a great role to be cast in. I certainly liked the idea of playing the first woman councillor in a northern town that wasn't used to such a thing, and Alan's writing ensured the drama was a huge hit. We made thirty one-hour episodes in all, over two years.

And with the role of Independent Councillor Sarah Danby, I found that – as stage and cinema audiences had before – television viewers would accept me in a long-running serious drama. They wouldn't always expect me to play comedy. Don't forget I had just come out of *Meet the Wife*, which had been a huge comedy success for the BBC. And I have Alan Plater to thank for helping me make that great leap from TV comedy to TV drama.

Now of course I have a third Alan – Alan J. W. Bell who produces and directs *Last of the Summer Wine*. But more of him elsewhere in this book.

The only real problem I encountered when *The First Lady* was broadcast – and perhaps 'problem' is too big a word for it – was that some viewers really thought I was a councillor and started writing to me to help sort out some of their local problems. One person wanted me to organise a new sewer pipe to be laid in a street, while another complained about the man next door keeping pigs even though the council had told him to remove them!

ALAN PLATER

One day in or around 1968 I had a telephone call from David Rose, the founder-producer of *Z Cars*, a good friend to this day and a man who revolutionised British television drama during his years at BBC Pebble Mill and Channel 4. David is a producer of the old school, meaning he trusts writers. On this occasion he trusted me with an offer that ran: 'Would you like to create a drama series for Thora Hird?'

I think I said something like: 'Er …'

I certainly hesitated. At the time Thora was best known for her work in *Meet the Wife* with Freddie Frinton, and I saw myself as a gritty northern realist, dedicated to bringing down capitalism within the next fortnight at the latest. Writing for Thora Hird didn't feel like a major step towards the revolution. David's offer seemed, at best, like a great leap sideways. Then I realised that inside the comic performer was a gritty northern woman – indeed, that's why she was funny. The healthiest kind of laughter comes from a recognition of truth. We don't laugh at lies, which is why so few politicians are funny. I met the situation head-on by proposing a series with Thora as a gritty northern councillor in a gritty northern town. Initially I suggested she be a renegade in the Labour Party – a sort of Barbara Castle figure who spent more time fighting with her own colleagues than with the Tories. The BBC hierarchy went a little pale and said: 'We have to be terribly careful about political balance. Couldn't she be an Independent?'

The notion of an Independent councillor in the sort of town I had in mind (we eventually filmed in Barnsley) was lunacy of a high order. I fought passionately for my principles for an hour or so and then gave way. Subsequently there arrived on our screens The First Lady, AKA Sarah Danby, Independent Councillor in the gritty northern town of Furness which, when we saw it, looked a bit like Barnsley, for obvious reasons. In dramatic terms I made an interesting discovery. As an Independent, Sarah could believe anything she wanted to believe. I daresay that's what the word means. In one of my episodes she found common cause with a Communist shop steward, at a time when Harold Wilson would have deported all CP members if he could have found some place nasty enough. The story caused a few twitches in the BBC hierarchy but the viewers took it in their stride, as viewers do. They're all independents too. I have no idea how the series would look today – indeed, I have no idea whether any of the episodes survived the cullings of the 1960s and 1970s. What I do remember is that Thora was terrific, in rehearsal, in performance and in the bar afterwards. She is a supreme teller of theatrical tales, most of which contain a deal of wisdom if you pay proper attention, especially on the subject of comedy. She taught me more than I realised at the time.

Viewed from this distance – a third of a century later, no less – it seems fair to claim *The First Lady* as a crucial stepping stone in Thora's career, from the knockabout fun of *Meet the Wife* to the glory days with Alan Bennett. The last time I spoke to her, at a BAFTA ceremony a few years ago, she said: 'Where would I be without my two Alans?' Compliments don't come any prettier than that and the only proper response is: where would any writers be without performers of the sublime quality of Dame Thora Hird?

Cream Cracker Under the Settee (1987, BBC)

Thora plays Doris, the incapacitated geriatric who refuses to be put in a home, in Alan Bennett's powerful and award-winning *Talking Heads* monologue, 'Cream Cracker Under the Settee'.

I don't think there's anyone in this country who hasn't at some stage been moved to laughter or tears by the works of Alan Bennett. Even actors who sit and read his scripts can be deeply moved. I know I always have been. I remember getting the script for Alan's 'Cream Cracker Under the Settee' and from page one I knew it would be difficult to do without crying. But at the back of my mind I could hear my dear father directing me, telling me that if you show too much emotion you won't get the audience as moved. I clung on to that thought. Until the first day of rehearsals, that is. By page eleven I could hardly speak. I apologised to the director Stuart Burge, who was holding back the tears himself.

The play, you might remember, was about an elderly woman who doesn't want to be forced to go into a home. Well, if I tell you the number of letters I received from people offering me to come and live with them ... The funny thing was that they were all addressed to Thora Hird and not my character Doris.

Oh, 'Cream Cracker' was a wonderful piece to work on – a forty-five-minute monologue where every syllable of every word had been written by Alan for a reason – and I was so proud that as a result of the production I was nominated for a British Academy Award for Best Actress. It was a great honour, especially aged 77.

I'll never forget the night of the awards. I was sitting at the table at the Grosvenor House with Jan and Scottie as Peter Davison read out the nominees and they played the clips. I wasn't really expecting to win. I had been nominated before and hadn't won and that particular night I was up against very stiff acting competition. And then Peter opened the envelope and announced: 'And the winner is ... Thora Hird in "Cream Cracker Under the Settee".' The place went mad. Everyone was on their feet. I was so moved and thankful for their ovation but especially thankful to dear Alan Bennett without whom I would never have won the award.

Meet the Wife (1964-66, BBC)

In a roundabout sort of way, my success with *Meet the Wife* came about because of my dear brother Nev. He was a funny man and Scottie and I always encouraged him to write. At the end of 1961 I think it was, I was being booked to star in a show for the next summer. The play I was presented with was awful. Brother Nev had written something that I thought was very funny and I said I would present it to the producer. So as not to look as though he was trading on the family name, we took some of my late Dad's name James Henry and my mother's maiden name Meyer and told the

RONALD WOLFE

I was called by theatrical impresario George Black, who said he had a show in Blackpool that he wanted myself and my co-writer Ronald Chesney to rewrite for him. We said we were too busy and then, after an expensive lunch in Mayfair, suddenly found time.

The show starred Thora Hird and Freddie Frinton. I'd never seen Thora on stage before and she was magnificent with a fantastic rapport with the audience. The on-stage chemistry between Thora and Freddie gave Chesney and me the idea to write our next TV series around them.

We went to some BBC executives and were shattered by their reaction. 'Thora Hird,' they said. 'Why on earth do you want to write for that clapped-out performer?'

Then Bill Cotton came to our rescue. He was making his way up the executive ladder and had the authority to commission a pilot show for Thora Hird. And he did. We thought that from then on in, all would be smooth sailing – but no way. We innocently assumed that the show would be recorded in one of the beautifully equipped studios at the Television Centre at White City. But no. 'They' said there was no room for us in London and we were sent to do the show in Birmingham. And not even in a proper studio.

We were allocated a disused cinema that was being used as a makeshift studio in a remote suburb. The atmosphere was tacky and the equipment was faulty. Our director was a film director who, though successful in films, had never directed a television show, and had never been on a training course. Oh, and when we asked the camera crew if they had any experience of sitcoms, they told us they usually did *Gardening Club*.

Eventually the show was recorded but I feared the worst, even though the show was good and Thora gave the performance of her life.

The story was simple. Thora was married to plumber Fred and for their twenty-fifth anniversary, now that they had a bit of money, she wanted a new bed. The first night in the new bed they had a row. Fred went off to sleep in the spare room – in the old bed – taking most of the blankets with him. Thora, looking for more blankets, finds Fred's anniversary present and a love-letter, probably the only one he has ever written. Brushing away a tear, Thora tiptoes into the spare room and creeps into the old bed to snuggle up next to Fred. And that's how we left them, as we found them, at the start of the show.

The public response was terrific and begrudgingly we got one series out of the BBC. When they realised how it had been received they renegotiated very quickly. We did forty shows in the end and every one was a joy. Thanks to Thora, who of all the ladies I've worked with, was the easiest to get along with.

Helplessly in love, Thora and Freddie Frinton star as Thora and Freddie Blacklock in one of the BBC's biggest comedy successes of the 1960s, *Meet the Wife*. On average the show pulled in around fifteen million viewers a week and helped make Thora a household name.

show they wanted us to record. How we ever got through it I really don't know. We had to film it at the BBC studios in Birmingham. Poor Freddie had been rehearsing the pilot during the days and appearing in pantomime in the evenings. He was so exhausted he could hardly stay awake and with most of the action – if you will excuse the expression – taking place in a bed (the pilot was called *The Bed*), I had terrible trouble keeping him awake. Honestly, he kept dropping off and I had to politely but firmly nudge him in the ribs to bring him back to life again.

producer that the writer was a new chap called Henry J. Meyer. It didn't seem to matter whose name was on the script. The producer loved it, and a few months later we were rehearsing *The Best Laid Schemes* for a summer season at Blackpool in 1962.

In the show my husband was played by variety actor Freddie Frinton. We hit it off straightaway and, after a successful season up north, took the show for a season to Torquay where the writers Ronald Chesney and Ronald Wolfe came to see it. They had just scored a huge success with *The Rag Trade* with Reg Varney and a very young Barbara Windsor and had written a pilot

Parkinson (1999, BBC)

The compliments you get in life that mean the most to an actor or an actress often come from within the business itself. I'm not talking about the artificial smiles and back-patting that goes on at so many show-business bashes – you can tell if those are meant or not – but the really heartfelt compliments. Such as the one Victoria Wood paid me when she presented me with a British Comedy Award in December 1998. She

said at the time, live on television, that she watched 'Waiting for the Telegram' and cried. Even though she knew it was her friend Thora acting, she still cried. And that, she said, was the sign of good acting. Now I'm not telling you this to swank or sound big-headed. Far from it. I find such compliments can be a bit embarrassing, but I was reminded of her thoughts when I appeared on the *Parkinson* show in early 1999.

Thora talking to host Michael Parkinson when she appeared on his show in February 1999.

They showed an extract from 'Waiting for the Telegram' and – even though I was sitting next to Michael Parkinson and in front of an audience, all of whom could see me in real life and then see me acting on the screen – when the lights came back up again I could see tears in the eyes of several of them, including two six-foot members of the crew. Even Parky wiped his eye. It was the bit where Violet is telling the young male nurse about the war and her young man, whom she loved and who was about to leave to go to France, who wanted to make love to her on his last night. And Violet hadn't let him.

Then there's a pause and she says, 'I should have let him, shouldn't I?' And Violet manages not to break down. Just. Which sets the viewers off, you see.

Well, it would be wrong for me to be talking about compliments without dishing one out to someone else. And since I'm talking about the *Parkinson* show, it's him who gets it, because he's always been one of the most natural interviewers on television and as well as enjoying appearing on his show, I've always thoroughly enjoyed watching it too. Now how's that for a compliment!

This Is Your Life – TWICE!

They say that a cat has nine lives. Well, I haven't had as many as that, but if *This Is Your Life* is anything to go by, I've had two so far. Yes, I've been caught out twice by the man with the red book. The first time was back in the 1960s when my daughter Jan and I had been asked to take part in setting up David Frost to be 'done'.

Quite an elaborate scheme was hatched whereby I persuaded David that as an up-and-coming television producer he had a responsibility to watch programmes being filmed, whether it be sport, news, light entertainment and so on. He seemed to agree and before he knew it I said that we should go and sit in the audience of

This Is Your Life during one of its filmings. He wasn't keen at all. But I finally persuaded him and managed to get him to the studios in Shepherds Bush at the agreed time. Even though we were supposed to be secret guests, we ended up sitting in the front row.

The show began and out from behind the curtains came Eamonn Andrews. Everyone clapped and he started his spiel. He was standing right in front of us and David kept looking round to see who might be there to be caught out. I tried not to laugh. Then Eamonn came and introduced us to the audience. There was great applause as he called out David's name, then mine, then Janette's. He said to David: 'Did she have a lot of trouble getting you here tonight?'

'Well yes, actually she did,' he replied. I was beaming.

'Never mind,' said Eamonn, 'the most important thing is that she got you here so that I can say tonight, *this is your life ...*'

And at that point he turned towards me and shoved the red book right under my nose as he added the words: '... Thora Hird!'

'No, it's not,' I argued. 'It's his!' But it wasn't. It was mine and I hadn't tricked David, he had tricked me.

Well, that would be that, I thought. And I was wrong. Over thirty years later, I'm up in Holmfirth on location with *Last of the Summer Wine*, standing outside the house that doubles for my cottage in the show, filming a piece with my screen husband Gordon Wharmby and a few others, including Peter Sallis who plays Clegg. Suddenly Michael Aspel appears and I think, I wonder who he could be here for. It can't be me, they've done me already. But I was wrong again. Out came the magic words: 'Tonight, Thora Hird, this

For once Edie Pegden is speechless as, while filming on location for *Summer Wine*, Thora gets caught out by Michael Aspel – the man with the red book – for *This Is Your Life*.

is your life!' Well, I say 'out came the magic words' but truthfully they didn't come out quite right and Michael appeared to say 'Dora Hird, this is your life!' So to be sure, they filmed that bit again. But it was still all a great surprise.

I've since discovered that several people have had more than one red book tribute over the years. I know Norman Wisdom has had two and I think dear Harry Secombe had three. But apparently they like to leave at least ten years between doing someone again. So if I make it to 100, I'll keep a look out over my shoulder every time I'm out in my bath chair!

PETER SALLIS

Believe it or not, after more than fifteen years since Thora joined *Summer Wine*, I have never actually shared a scene with her. Well, I wouldn't do really, I suppose. The menfolk are always trying to escape the women – particularly the forthright and bossy Edie.

Yet Thora and I always have a good laugh together when we are off-set. When she first joined the team we invented this imaginary friendship between the two of us which had, we told people, started with us walking arm in arm along the bank of a canal in Bruges. I'm not sure there is even a canal at Bruges, but that didn't seem to matter. We proclaimed how right we were for each other. Each time we told the story the setting shifted, from Bruges to Paris to Brussels and, once, even Amsterdam. One day we let it slip that the friendship had started when we were both just five! No one pointed out that I wasn't even born when Thora was five! It was all a bit of fun.

I remember we were all outside the cottage that doubles for Edie's home one day when suddenly Michael Aspel turned up and before we knew it had thrust his red book in front of her announcing: 'Thora Hird, this is your life!' At least that's what he meant to say. It actually sounded like 'Dora Hird', and he had to record his entrance again. It was still a great surprise to us all and as they whisked her away, I remember shouting out: 'Take me with you!' They cut that bit out!

While we may not have worked closely together I can say that Thora is a great actress and I have great admiration for her. Particularly for her enormous courage coupled with her determination not to allow her increasing immobility to get in the way of her work. That's the sign of a real professional.

Lost for Words (1999, YORKSHIRE TELEVISION)

Immediately after filming Alan Bennett's 'Waiting for the Telegram', I started work on a most touching drama called *Lost for Words*, in the spring of 1998. Yet I had actually been approached about *Lost for Words* a few years before that by the writer Deric Longden. I had appeared in his television play, *Wide Eyed and Legless*, with Julie Walters and Jim Broadbent. This was based on life with Deric's first wife, who developed ME and eventually died. In it I played the senile old mother. Deric came to see me when I was on location in Huddersfield making *Last of the Summer Wine* and told me he had written another play, this time about his mother and the relationship with her son as she suffers three strokes before dying.

Deric insisted no one else could play the part but me and wanted to put my name forward with my agreement. I refused point blank. I didn't want my name used in connection with it in case it influenced any production company in either a positive or negative way. That wouldn't be right.

A year went by before Deric came back to see me and I asked how it was going.

He said he had been searching for finance and promised he had never used my name, and then showed me a letter from a potential investor which read: 'If you can get Thora Hird interested, we'll buy it.' I asked for a copy of the play to read, and cried for most of the day. It was wonderful.

And that's how I came to be in it.

Making the drama was thoroughly enjoyable if hard work. There were so many speaking parts in it and the set

Thora with Pete Postlethwaite in Yorkshire Television's 1999 drama *Lost for Words*.

PETE POSTLETHWAITE
Speaking in 1998

Lost for Words was quite emotionally demanding. The story was very near to Thora's heart and you could see at times it was pretty heart-wrenching for her. But it was also excruciatingly funny and I couldn't get through scenes sometimes. It's just the way this extraordinary magician of a lady can deliver a line without it being 'bashed on the head'. It doesn't seem like she's making a joke but it's desperately funny coming from her.

Thora and I had a fantastic relationship making *Lost for Words*. During filming we sat and had a drink and talked in the evenings. My own mum was eighty-five at the time and of the same northern ilk – one of those ladies who has that indomitable spirit. They've borne a lot in their lives with extraordinary grace and goodwill. Certainly, in the later years of her life, there's an amazing similarity. When I worked with Thora I could actually have been talking to my own mum.

was always busy with actors and crew. I was having problems with my legs so they gave me a double and one day she brought in some photos of her when she was a stripper, as a much younger woman, you understand. 'Well', I said, a little taken aback, 'I could never have doubled for you!'

The days were long – I was up at half five every morning – but each day I thanked God not only to be alive but to have the chance to be in something so special at my age.

Oh, there was one star who outshone us all in the play if some are to be believed. If you've seen *Lost for Words*, you'll remember that I have a cat. There was one scene where I had to give it a bath. Luckily the cat enjoyed a bath so I didn't get scratched. The cat's owner was there all the time and she used to call out to it: 'Oh, you are a clever one, you have done well! Now Thora will tell you how good you've been and what a big star you are.' I turned and smiled and politely said: 'Be careful, my dear, he'll want top billing next!'

DERIC LONGDEN
Speaking in 1998

My mother's eccentricity was something the family took for granted. It had always been there – her inventive way with words and the strange logic that was ever-so-slightly twisted. We became used to her ways and Pete took it all calmly in his stride as Thora lived the part. In fact Thora almost is my mother. I remember sitting with her during a break in filming. The crew had gone for lunch, but Thora remained on the set, a loving re-creation of my mother's lounge. She ate a cream cake and I sat at her feet, on the hearth. As we talked, I was suddenly transported back some twenty years or so. This was my mother, this was her house. It was all quite disturbing. The film has the same effect on me. It has put me through the wringer with its mixture of laughter and tears. Just like life, really.

Waiting for the Telegram (1998, BBC)

When Alan Bennett's script for his *Talking Heads* monologue, 'Waiting for the Telegram', arrived on my doorstep I was so excited. He told me he had written it especially for me. That really was a great compliment. I sat down, opened the envelope, pulled out the script, turned the page and read the first line: 'I saw this feller's what-do-you-call-it today …' and further down the page, 'Now, Violet, was the penis erect?' I thought to myself, 'My goodness, if it wasn't Alan writing this, I'd never do it.'

I kept thinking, 'I can't do this, I just can't.' And then I got to thinking about the words and what he was trying to get at. It's the nurse that asks about the erect penis but because it's a monologue, I'm the one that has to recall the story. And then I concentrated on how I could say the lines without being embarrassed. I realised that in some old people's homes and hospitals it may happen from time to time and that you'd get an old lady saying to another, 'I saw this bloke's what-do-you-call-it this morning ...' And it was so matter-of-fact, funny almost, that the more I tried it the easier it became to say. My character Violet was like many elderly people. She wasn't easily shocked. For that matter, neither am I. And anyway, I thought, it's Alan Bennett, so I'm sure people won't mind.

Alan writes truthfully, not dirtily for the sake of it. Within a few days of 'Waiting for the Telegram' being broadcast I had four plays sent to me. The first one had a four-letter word on the second page. The others weren't much better. I sent them back.

Looking back now, I realise how lucky I was to be offered the monologue. What a wonderful piece of writing about missed opportunity! Poor Violet sending away the man she loves without allowing him to make love to her, and him being lost in the war. It said so much about life on so many different levels and when I won the BAFTA for it, I thought this isn't just for me or for Alan, it's for so many people in our country who found themselves in a situation similar to Violet's and for our great men who gave their lives for our freedom. God bless them all!

Thora as Violet in 'Waiting for the Telegram' from the BBC's 1998 Talking Heads series.

© BBC 1998

Dinnerladies (1998, BBC)

Victoria Wood is a very funny lady and she's very talented too. I was so delighted to see her win two British Comedy Awards in the year 2000, especially after she had presented me with one two years earlier. I sat and watched the show on television that

night and I was so proud for her and of her. She won one of the awards for *Dinnerladies*, which most people don't realise she actually wrote entirely by herself.

Victoria was very kind about me a couple of years ago. She said: 'I first worked with Thora in 1994 when she played Duncan Preston's mother in *Pat and Margaret*. I had written to her ten years earlier when I was doing my sketch show *As Seen on TV*, but 1994 was the first year she had free.' Well, I'm delighted she persisted because I have had the chance to work with Victoria a couple of times over the past seven or eight years and they've always been such fun.

She gave me a little cameo role in *Dinnerladies* back in the first series in 1998. There was Eric Sykes, myself and Dora Bryan brought on as the parents of some of the characters. We only had a few lines each but it was worth it. My first line was to Celia Imrie.

'Did you get that skirt from a catalogue?' I asked.

'No,' she protested.

'Pity,' I said. 'You could have sent it back.' It was very funny.

Dora Bryan went to the wardrobe department to find a cap to go with the track suit she was wearing – for the part, of course. She picked one that I'd recently worn in *Last of the Summer Wine*. She came on set and I said: 'You've got my bloody hat on.'

'Yes, I know,' she said, 'but they've said you're not wearing it any more.'

Which worried me a little. I thought, is there something no one is telling me? I needn't have worried. I've been back to Yorkshire for three more seasons of *Summer Wine* since, and I'm hoping to go up for more, cap or no cap.

Pat and Margaret (1994, BBC)

When I first started out in this business, it was often a bit of a handicap being northern, or at least sounding too northern. It was easier for

comedians – people seemed to think it enhanced the humour. But straight acting was another thing entirely. Of course, all that changed when 'gritty

Thora with Victoria Wood and Duncan Preston, during the shooting of the 1994 comedy film *Pat and Margaret*.

© Express Syndication

VICTORIA WOOD OBE

I have been a fan of Thora since the days of *Meet the Wife*, and *The First Lady*, but I didn't actually get to work with her until 1994, when we did *Pat and Margaret*. I think I had written to her ten years earlier, but that was the first date she had free. I had written the part of a domineering mother, who keeps her illiterate son, Jim, played by Duncan Preston, under her thumb, until he finally breaks free and reveals he has in fact had a sex life with his waitress girlfriend, Margaret. We filmed that scene at the top of a very steep hill in a Lancashire town. Thora, tiny in a flowered pinny, is doing disgusting things to the front gate with a feather duster, and Duncan stands defiantly outside the house with his arm round Margaret. On hearing the news that Jim and Margaret haven't just been playing whist, the mother recoils. Thora is good at recoiling, especially the northern kind.

'A sex life?' she cries. 'Where have you had it?'

'On your bed,' replies Jim simply.

Further top-class recoilment, perfectly timed pause. 'Not on the eiderdown!'

Pat and Margaret was known for the rest of the filming as the 'Not on the Eiderdown' show. I was very struck by Thora's attitude to work and her place in the business. She had a lot of respect for everyone else on the shoot – she didn't demand any special treatment, she didn't go around acting the part of the lovable old character, she just got on with it. But everyone did give her special treatment, because she was special.

---

realism' became the phrase everyone talked about in the 1950s and 1960s, with plays like John Osborne's *Look Back in Anger* and those great films, *Saturday Night and Sunday Morning* and *A Kind of Loving*. I've never tried to hide my accent, unless the part demanded it of course. Indeed, most people who hear my voice assume I still live in my home town of Morecambe. They get such a shock when I tell them I've been living in London since 1947!

Victoria Wood is a northerner and what a great writer and actress she is. We finally got the chance to work together in 1994 on her television film *Pat and Margaret*. I played the overbearing and possessive mother to my slightly backward son played by Duncan Preston. We shared a laugh on and off the set on more than one occasion.

In one scene I had to answer the telephone, pretend to be listening and put it back. His line was: 'Was that Margaret?'

And mine was, 'No. It was your Auntie Rene. She wants some more of that wool. Hey! Your ticket's hanging out.'

The cameraman wanted to shoot the shot again from a different angle but didn't need the sound. Duncan didn't know that, so imagine his face when it came to my line again and I said: 'No, it was your Auntie Rene. She wants some more of that wool. Hey! – your flies are open!'

He stood there stuttering and trying to compose himself. He thought he'd spoiled the shot and kept apologising to the director. Poor Duncan! We did have a laugh over that one.

Last of the Summer Wine (1985 ONWARDS, BBC)

I've said many times that I was delighted when I was approached to be in *Last of the Summer Wine* because I truly always have been a fan of the show. I was only ever supposed to play a cameo role in the feature-length episode 'Uncle of the Bride' in 1986. But then the director, Alan J. W. Bell, asked me to come back for a bit more

Thora is presented with her own 'director's' chair by some of the *Summer Wine* crew.

and then a bit more and now over fifteen years later I'm still in the show. And I love it. I do get concerned that some viewers think I really am like the battle-axe Edie Pegden that I play in the show, and on more than one occasion I've been stopped in the street and asked why I treat my husband so badly. I carefully point out that I'm acting the words of the writer and that I'm not like that at all.

One of the delights of the show is going back to Holmfirth every year, which really is the most beautiful of Yorkshire towns. I don't deny that on a wet and cold day, being stuck in our caravan can get a little depressing, but overall it's such fun. I used to share a caravan with Kathy Staff and Jane Freeman – Freeman Hardy and Willis, they nicknamed us. And with my arthritis they've always been so kind to me, making sure I'm warm and have a cup of tea to hand. I'm sad that Kathy's left after all these years, but isn't

DORA BRYAN

Thora and I go back ever such a long way. I think we first worked together over fifty years ago. She would know. She's got a better memory than me. We used to do so many films in those days. She used to play the chars and landladies. I used to play the tarts or barmaids! Occasionally I played a waitress, if things went really up-market.

I seem to remember our first film together being the comedy, *The Cure for Love* in 1949 with Robert Donat. I played the young female lead. Isn't it funny that over half a century later, Thora and I are working together again on *Last of the Summer Wine*? We still get on so famously well. Well, we would do. We both come from the same part of the world – Lancashire. Thora comes from Morecambe – the posh end – and I come from Oldham.

We sit in our caravan on location in the Yorkshire hills singing songs from the old days.

When we have a few hours off I push her in her wheelchair through Huddersfield Market. Like the Queen Mother and her lady-in-waiting, with everyone handing her flowers, which she passes behind, to me. I'll need to go back to the market very soon. That's where Thora and I get our nighties from!

She's a wonderful woman, Thora, and I love her greatly.

it wonderful to see her back in *Crossroads* again.

The outdoor scenery may not have changed much over the years, but certainly the way we make the show when we are indoors has. We used to record the interiors – as we call them – at BBC studios in front of an audience. Now we film the interiors in a film studio, like Pinewood, Elstree or Shepperton, and when it's all cut together we play the show to an audience and sit with them while their laughter is recorded and added to the soundtrack.

Some of the cast come along and do a bit of a 'warm-up' first, a sketch or a song. I used to do a 'bit of business' with Gordon Wharmby who plays my husband, Wesley. You know the sort of

ALAN J. W. BELL

Edie Pegden – sister to new character Seymour Utterthwaite and of course the bride's mother – wasn't a big part, but it was a good one. The big problem was, who could I get to play her who would make the character funny and also be different from the tough Yorkshire women like Nora Batty, Ivy and Pearl, who were already firmly established in the series. My wife immediately suggested Thora Hird. I embraced this suggestion with my usual respect and told her not to be silly and to mind her own business. There was no way that Thora Hird would join us to play such a relatively small part in a long-running series. But my wife was insistent. She had seen Thora being interviewed on television when she had just finished *In Loving Memory*, and had picked up the fact that Thora admired the Yorkshire countryside and had very fond memories of working there.

With nothing to lose, I tentatively rang Felix de Wolfe, Thora's agent, and he immediately said that he would ask her. He called back straightaway and said that she would be delighted to be with us. From that moment on, the production rose in stature and we were making a really special 'special'.

Although Thora's career has spanned the whole spectrum of theatre, film and television, it is in front of a camera that she feels most comfortable. She understands the business of filming and immediately identified me as having been a film editor. 'I can always tell, love. You don't shoot the scene from every angle, then work out how it cuts later.' Like the late Bill Owen, she knows how to play a scene completely out of order and in bits, but always with the continuity of her performance clearly in mind and a gifted understanding of the script. Watching her work to the camera is an object lesson to all would-be film actors – and some who have made it to the top too soon.

Thora was truly wonderful as Edie, and the viewing figures showed, quite clearly, that she brought to the programme a legion of devoted fans – including senior management on the sixth floor at the BBC's Television Centre: 'Can you try and keep Thora Hird in the series? She is marvellous.' Getting Thora Hird to be a guest star in a TV movie is one thing, but to ask her to join the series as a regular is another. But as we had all got on superbly well working together, I asked her. Thora Hird joined the series as a regular 'special guest star' playing Edie and in 2001, aged ninety, she is still working with us and still making us laugh. Never late on the set (strict training from her director father), and always putting her pain aside (and she has a lot of that now, in her later years) to make her performance in front of the camera as funny as possible. We all love her.

The infamous
Summer Wine ladies'
coffee mornings, as
Thora is joined by
fellow cast members:
(back row)
Juliette Kaplan,
Jane Freeman,
Kathy Staff
(front row)
Dora Bryan and
Sarah Thomas.

SARAH THOMAS

When I heard that I had been cast as Thora's daughter in *Last of the Summer Wine* I was absolutely thrilled. She had long been one of my idols but to become her screen daughter was pretty amazing! That was sixteen years ago and I consider myself very lucky and extremely privileged to have been playing Glenda all this time.

Of course when we first met on the set Thora was absolutely charming. Over the years we have become really good friends and I love her dearly. Our scenes together are my favourite and we have a lot of fun playing them. We have found ourselves in that red car of Edie's at various times: on top of a man-made hill; going the wrong way down a one-way street; on a railway line and even driving at speed on to a vehicle carrier – more stunts than the average thriller movie but a lot more laughs with Thora.

Watching Thora working is always a pleasure and a learning experience. When she was memorising the lines for Alan Bennett's 'Waiting for the Telegram', we were on location and Thora would 'do' bits of the monologue in her caravan. I knew the script quite well by the time it was transmitted. I still watched it with tears running down my face. It was so truthful, moving and real.

One day I shall never forget was a couple of years ago when Thora came out of hospital, against the wishes of her doctor, in order to complete her scenes in *Last of the Summer Wine*. She was driven to Pinewood Studios by ambulance, with a nurse in attendance; she and I filmed for three hours and then she went back to her bed in hospital. A true professional, she never complains, never asks for special favours but is always one of the girls.

Thora makes a pre-*Summer Wine* appearance with Bill Owen, before his Compo days, for the 1960s BBC radio series, *There's One Born Every Minute*.

thing. He'd be quietly having a moan about me to the audience and then from the corner of the stage I shouted out, 'I heard that.' Boy, did we get a laugh on that one. Nowadays, being a little less mobile, I just sit for a few minutes and talk to the audience about the making of the show.

Every year I phone up Alan and tell him that I think I'm just not up to doing another series and each time he says: 'I'm not listening, Thora.' He doesn't mean it in a rude way. He just loves the show and cares about his cast. And I'm thankful he pushes me a bit to do it, because working on the show has been one of the happiest experiences of my career and I'd like to continue doing it for as long as I can.

TOM OWEN

Perhaps not all of us know that my father worked with Thora on numerous occasions over the years prior to *Last of the Summer Wine* but only very rarely shared a scene on film, television or radio. So, of course they had met each other before finally acting together when Thora joined *Last of the Summer Wine*.

I fondly recall my father often mentioning Thora when he returned from filming yet another series of *Summer Wine*, and I knew that he had a great respect for her as an actress and always enjoyed her company. As her arthritis took hold, he marvelled at the way Thora coped with it and managed to have all the company in fits of laughter in spite of her pain.

His death and my sudden arrival in *Last of the Summer Wine* has been well chronicled, and I know that he would be thrilled to know that not only is the series carrying on but with Thora very much at the helm! She is in his words 'a true professional' – one of the very few left. It was certainly difficult enough for me for obvious reasons joining the world's longest-running comedy series but to be working with *the* Thora Hird … that was really scary! Of course, I needn't have worried. The entire cast, but in particular Thora, went out of their way to help and support me.

It came to light while we were making the last series that Thora adored eating trout. Now I am the world's keenest fly fisherman and whenever I have a day off from filming, I can be found on the bank of a lake about twenty miles away from Holmfirth where *Summer Wine* is made. When Thora heard of my passion for fishing, we struck a deal – she would provide the champagne if I provided the trout! Consequently, we would have a wonderful dinner at the Huddersfield Hotel, Thora with her trout and me with my champagne!

CHAPTER 4

Family

Thora and Her Brother Neville

My brother Neville – whom I always used to call Our Nev – and I were both born on a Sunday, he just before morning service and me just before evening service. Not on the same Sunday, you understand. He was a year older than me and we also had a sister Olga who was fifteen months older than him.

We were always close, right from the word go. He was my playmate, my protector and most of all, my best friend. We used to play cowboys, as young children. We called ourselves Tom and Mary Whitfield – though I

Thora with her older brother Neville dressed up for another piece of play-acting in one of their father's shows at the Royalty Theatre, Morecambe around 1915.

couldn't tell you why – and we pretended that our horsehair couch was our trusted steed. We learned to play the piano together and practised for an hour every day. Nev was more musical and had a violin, a guitar and a flexatone. I wonder how many of you are old enough to remember one of those! My father and mother were musical too. What happy Sunday afternoons we spent together with Dad on the banjo, Nev on the violin, Mother singing and me doing my best on the piano. I'm not looking through rose-coloured spectacles, you know, they really were great days.

Nev and I stayed so close all our lives and in the 1960s he wrote a hilarious stage farce, *The Best Laid Schemes*, which was a huge success and led to my television show *Meet the Wife* being produced. I know I have so much to be thankful to him for.

Dear Nev died in May 1975. It was a Saturday and I had to start a new comedy play in Brighton on the Monday. It was the only time in my whole career I was 'off' from a play. Our Nev would probably have told me to go on if he could have been heard. That's what he was like. Always thinking of his little sister.

Thora takes time off for a cup of tea and a chat as she visits brother Neville (right) and one of his work colleagues – engineers for the Lancashire local authority. Years later Neville turned his full attention to writing stage plays, with his first, *The Best Laid Schemes*, a huge hit for him and for Thora, who appeared in it.

Wedding Day

I first met Scottie the night they reopened the Winter Gardens at Morecambe in 1933. I was so happy to be there because I'd stood on the promenade earlier that year and watched it burn down. I say 'first met' Scottie, but really it was a case of when I first saw him. He was a drummer in the orchestra and a jolly good one too. That's not why I took a shine to him. Don't ask me what it was. Who really knows about these things? All I know is that while there was no flash of thunder, I did feel warm inside and that warmth grew as we started 'going out' together.

We saw each other every day for three years before we became engaged. We went to see his father in Scotland. Scottie already knew my parents – he'd been eating dinner at our house for the past three years! His father was known as 'the chief' and he was a wonderful

man. After Scottie and I were married he came to live with us, and in his eyes I could do no wrong. He always stuck up for me. It wasn't all one-sided, though. My mother always used to stick up for Scottie.

During our courtship, I was working in the theatre and Scottie was in the orchestra, as often as not, at another venue. We would meet up after our respective curtains came down. If he was at the Royalty and their curtain was down first he would walk over to the Winter Gardens to collect me. And of course vice versa.

It was on one of those walks that my Scottie, who was quite an undemonstrative man, stopped me by what looked like a mound of dug earth and said: 'Did you ever think you would have to get married?'

I was shocked. 'Certainly not!'

Thora and her groom James 'Scottie' Scott on their wedding day in Morecambe in 1936, flanked by Thora's mother Mary and father James.

'Well, you'll have to now,' he laughed, 'because this is going to be our house!'

I cried with happiness and romantically imagined how our new home would turn out, just as a cow walked past and left its 'calling card' in the foundations.

'Muck for luck', they say.

We called our home 'Prompt Corner' and it cost us the princely sum of four hundred and ninety-five pounds.

Thora and Baby Janette

Our first wedding anniversary arrived and Scottie and I were chatting about what we should get each other. Scottie laughed when he offered me a mink coat or a diamond solitaire. We weren't in debt but we didn't have any money either. In the end I settled for some

flowers and he got a shirt. There was one other thing we both wanted and we set about getting it that night.

Shortly afterwards I went to see my doctor, who lit up a cigarette as she asked me what was wrong. Can you imagine a doctor doing that today? I don't think so. I told her nothing was wrong and that I thought I was in an 'interesting condition'. She jumped up and hugged and congratulated me. She immediately put out her cigarette and asked, 'How far gone?'

'Three days,' I replied, quite happily.

'Three days!' she bellowed. 'Come back and see me in a couple of months. Three days, indeed!'

'But I'm telling you I'm three days pregnant. I just know I am.'

She laughed and bet me 100 cigarettes I was wrong. Well, I got my 100 cigarettes and a beautiful daughter, and my doctor delivered them both!

'How could you be so sure?' Doctor Jo asked me afterwards.

'Well,' I replied, 'when my Scottie makes his mind up to do a job, he makes sure he does it properly.'

And I've got my darling daughter Janette to prove it.

Janette's First Film Role

While I was making my second film, *Went the Day Well?*, I was filming by day and appearing on stage by night. At the time London was under constant threat of attack from the air, so Janette had to be packed off to Lancashire to be cared for by our nanny Vera when Scottie was on active service. It made living in London very lonely indeed for me, and even though I would be invited out to have a drink or a bite to eat after a show, it was no fun with my loved ones so far away. Any possible chance to see them was such a treat. But of course if I was working I couldn't ask a film director to halt production for a few hours while I met my family. There were so many of us in the same boat, we'd never have got anything made!

When Scottie was on leave from the RAF, he brought Janette down to London to visit me. While I was filming at Ealing Studios one day, Scottie took Janette out to play on the nearby common. Suddenly the director of the film found he needed a child for a bit part and wanted to use Jan. He sent two of his crew out to find them and I asked Scottie if he approved. He said yes, and that's how Janette started in the business. The bug bit and it wasn't until she started her own family many years later that she decided to give it all up. But not before she had worked on some great films with some great stars including Terry-Thomas, James Stewart and Marlene Dietrich. I've always been so proud of Janette. And I still am.

Thora and four-year-old daughter Janette in a publicity shot from the 1942 wartime classic *Went the Day Well?*

House Proud

I've lived in the same home since 1947. Not in Lancashire, as so many people naturally think, but actually in London. It wasn't easy pulling myself away from my northern roots, but with a seven-year film contract from Ealing under my belt and lots of stage work coming in, it seemed the sensible thing to do to move south. And I've been here ever since. Though, of course, my heart will always belong with my roots, in Morecambe. Anyway, Scottie and I moved into the little mews flat off Bayswater that we rented to begin with, before buying it in the 1950s. And that's where I still live today.

Now, I always like to keep everything spick and span and since I am a great lover of brass – handles, pots and pans and so on – when I wasn't working, it would be out with the Brasso, having a good polish.

Thora polishes the
door handle of the
home she moved
into after the war
and where she still
lives half a century
later. Notice the
'flower pot' in the
top right corner,
which was actually
an ammunition box
that Scottie brought
back after the war.

One day I was standing by my front door, my hair in curlers with a scarf wrapped round my head, wearing an old pinny and a pair of house slippers, polishing the door handle, when a Rolls-Royce drew up beside me. The window was wound down and a man who was smoking a cigar said in an American accent: 'I'm looking for Thora Hird. Do you know if she lives here?'

'Who wants her?' I asked politely. The man gave me his name and I realised I was face to face with a well known film producer. 'I'll just get her,' I stuttered. I dashed upstairs, took off the scarf, took out the curlers, brushed my hair, changed my dress and put on some posh shoes. Two minutes later I was back downstairs, welcoming the man into my home. To this day the film producer thinks he was met by Thora Hird's maid.

The End of the War

I was so happy once the war was over. Well, we all were, weren't we? Less for myself once the constant fear of bombing over our homes was out of the way, but more for the hope that our loved ones would come back alive from wherever they were serving.

When Scottie came home safe and sound from his active duty with the RAF it was a great opportunity to spend time as a family again. Janette came back home, and I cherished the long walks we could now take together in war-free London. Janette was becoming busier and busier as a young and blossoming actress. People sometimes ask me when she decided to become an actress. Well I don't think she ever did. I couldn't tell you when I did for that matter. I just did. I've always thought that no true actress ever decides to become one – she just is one.

Janette had the business almost bottle-fed to her from birth. I would take her to the theatre in her pram and leave her in the wings sleeping while I rehearsed, have a break and feed her, then go back to

Great Scotts! Thora enjoying the fresh air as she goes out for a walk with Scottie and daughter Janette after the end of World War II.

We Three, Great Scots!

rehearsing. It was obvious very early on that she wanted to perform.

I remember poor Scottie playing in a concert one night when Janette, who couldn't have been more than two or three, started giggling in the auditorium. He looked up and saw her standing in the aisle, pointing her toes and holding out the ends of her skirt, dancing to the music. What made it worse was that for fun the limeboy turned the spotlight on her instead of the soloist. Now you know where the phrase 'stealing the limelight' comes from. It could have been invented for my Janette!

At Home

We moved into our mews home in 1947, though we didn't actually buy it until 1955. Over half a century later, I still live here, even though I've got a small cottage next door to Jan in Chichester and she keeps begging me to move in there.

The funny thing about this flat of ours is that all through the war, while Scottie was serving with the RAF, I had taken to writing to Janette about the sort of home we would all move into after the war. It became a sort of serial story. Each week, I'd write a bit more and each week the house in the story would take some shape: the shape of a large loft that was going to be turned into a pretty flat with window boxes under windows that looked out on to a quiet cobbled lane where there were more stables and more windows and more window boxes and so on. And then this flat was to be near a park with ponds and sailing boats zig-zagging to miss the swans. These stories went on for months.

I don't know if it was fate, or if dreams really do come true if you wish for them hard enough, but would you believe that at the end of the war I

JANETTE SCOTT

If I was forced to pick out one word to describe my dad it would be 'nurturing', for he surely was. Maybe because his mother died when he was only six years old and his musician father had to take day and evening jobs to keep the family home together, my dad had to look after his youngest sisters for his father at that very early age.

We used to laugh and comment that children and animals always came to my dad with complete trust. When I was nine years old and under contract to Associated British Picture Corporation, it became clear that I was about to have a very busy career. Although I was in no way involved in the decision, Dad gave up his own career at the time to look after his two 'girls', Mum and me.

When I grew up and left home he turned his full concentration on my mother – protecting and cushioning her from the world, enabling her to do what she does best: being Thora Hird, the actress, the author, the amazing communicator for causes and charities. Dad was her personal manager and advisor, her home organiser and wonderful cook and loving husband (and not necessarily in that order!). He did everything, but never ever lost his own identity. Without doubt he was the master of his own house and no one would ever have called him 'Mr Thora Hird'. He was always Jimmy Scott.

A shot from the late 1960s as Thora takes a stroll up the mews she has lived in since 1947.

found such a flat. And I sent for Janette and she couldn't believe it. It was almost exactly like we had been talking about for so long. The mews flat was an old stable, it does look out on to a cobbled road and is just across the road from Hyde Park. And what was its name? Believe it or not, The Olde Lofte.

Scottie, Janette and Thora in their mews flat in London in 1955. Thora still lives there over half a century later after first moving in back in the late 1940s.

Dame Thora Hird OBE

In the autumn of 1992, Scottie and I arrived home from a cruise to the usual mountain of mail that we all get while we're away. I could be wrong but I often wonder if people send more post to you while you're away on purpose, because I never seem to get as much when I'm at home. Anyway, where was I? Oh, yes. One particular letter was printed on 10 Downing Street paper. I read it once and then read it again. It told me I was to become a Dame. I couldn't believe it. I hadn't long since received the OBE. I was sure they had made a mistake and even phoned up Downing Street to make sure it was right. They said it was. But they reminded me that I must not say a word about it until the announcement was made through the 'usual channels'.

I went to Buckingham Palace to receive my insignia on 30 November 1993. Jan and my grandchildren Daisy and James all flew in from the States. Dear Scottie gave up his place as you are only allowed three guests with you and he said that it was more important that the grandchildren came with me, especially as he had been there when I picked up my OBE.

When we went into the Palace there was a large orchestra playing at one end of the great hall.

A proud Dame Thora shows off her insignia outside Buckingham Palace with daughter Janette and grandchildren James and Daisy in November 1993.

They told me that I was to be 'first on', as it were. That made me nervous for a start. Having spent so many years in the theatre I felt like the curtain-raiser – the one who warms the audience up. Apparently I had to go on first. I was the only one being made a Dame that day.

I was also a little nervous because I knew I was supposed to curtsey to the Queen and even though I wanted to, I was having problems with my arthritis. The Palace gave me a page who escorted me up to Her Majesty. I needn't have worried. In the excitement of it all, I forgot the pain and managed the curtsey and was so pleased that I had.

Jan and the children were sitting in the front row and, as the Queen left, Daisy smiled at her and she smiled back. Oh, you should have seen Daisy's face! It was a picture. Worth the trip across just for that, she said to me afterwards. And knowing her the way I do, I'm sure it was.

Family Holidays

My family has always been the most precious and important thing to me, from being a little girl and loving my parents and my brother and sister, through to meeting the man of my dreams, Scottie – who I loved for every day of over fifty years of marriage – and of course, the love for my darling daughter, Janette.

And just when you think you've had your share of love, along come the grandchildren and it starts all over again. I've got two of the best. Well, I would say that, wouldn't I? Which grandmother wouldn't, except that in this case I really do believe it to be true. They are James and Daisy and they both live out in America where they were born.

James is a tall lad, over 6 foot, and how delighted I was that Jan decided to name him after my father, my father-in-law and my late husband. All James, they were. And now there's my grandson who's the fourth. James the fourth. Sounds like royalty. He'll like that.

Both James and Daisy are very musical – they get that from their late father, the singer Mel Tormé, and a little bit from my side of the family, I suppose.

Scottie and I used to go and visit the grandchildren as much as we could. It took a bit of organising, have to work around filming schedules and stage roles, but we used to miss them so much. I think we made over twenty visits during the fifteen years Jan was in Beverly Hills, bringing them up.

They're grown up now, but that doesn't stop me missing them and it doesn't stop me worrying too. Back in 1994 there was a terrible earthquake in Los Angeles and I couldn't sleep for worrying until I had heard from Jan that both of them were all right. Daisy told her that the walls of the condominium she was in had cracked

MEMORIES FROM JANETTE SCOTT

We were such a close-knit threesome – Mum, Dad and me. When I left England to marry and live in California in 1964 it was very difficult for all of us. But Mel Tormé lived in Beverly Hills. I loved him, and as his wife I was old-fashioned enough to believe a wife should go where her husband goes … But I was very homesick, especially when Daisy and James were born. I longed for them to spend as much time as possible with their grandparents. Mum and Dad came over and visited our home in Coldwater Canyon twenty-eight times between 1965 and 1978.

They would stay in the guest cottage by the swimming-pool. When they were due to arrive I would turn the temperature of the pool up into the high eighties (32° Celsius) and there in the very early morning, before breakfast, with the steam rising from the water, we would skinny-dip with the children. Wrapping ourselves in warm towelling robes we would breakfast on fresh Californian orange juice and tropical fruit; papayas and mangoes with fresh lime squeezed over them were Mum and Dad's favourites.

Mum played make-believe with Daisy from the moment Daisy could walk. My dad built a Wendy play-house for Daisy in the corner of the pool area and Mum and Dad would play all the time. Sometimes it was Daisy's country cottage and my mother would visit as various characters; often at other times it was a sweet shop and post office.

There were two wide steps leading down to the long living-room at Coldwater Canyon. It didn't take much imagination to make them into a stage, and shows were put on each week. Bearing in mind the extreme youth of the cast, these shows tended to be somewhat repetitive and full of 'showstoppers'. The cast was constantly giving way to 'encores' demanded by their adoring audience.

Mel's parents were great fun and would join in with the old Eddie Cantor songs. It's no surprise to me – with Mel's musical genius and Mum's extraordinary and brilliant acting genes – that Daisy and James entered the world of show business as the fourth generation.

and that all phone lines were down. Thank goodness for car phones, I thought. That's how she let us know she was safe. James phoned shortly afterwards and Scottie and I were able to relax again.

Daisy and James come over now whenever they can which, of course, is never going to be enough for a doting grandmother, is it? But they phone and write and we still laugh like we used to all those years ago when they were growing up.

MEMORIES FROM DAISY TORMÉ

I've been seeking the very back of my memory in an attempt to recall my first memory of my grandmother. I'm really not sure, and yet my first thought of her is always of how she was with me and how I looked at her as a small child. How can I put this? She would create with me. I remember countless days of playing very intricate scenes with her, using the miniature grocery shop set. It had everything! We could play for hours, each of us playing the customer and shop-owner several different ways by the time the game was over and it was time for a cup of tea. When my brother James and I would come over from America as very young children, she would take us on double-decker buses. We would always sit upstairs – and preferably in the front row – where we would see who could eat a Pacer sweet the slowest, which meant not chewing it, which was impossible. My mother always won that game; she'd just let it sit in her mouth and I'd think, 'How can she do that?'

The memories seem to be endless. When I was too young for me to remember exactly how old I really was, my grandparents came out to Los Angeles to visit us. It was during that trip that I began, as far as I can tell, learning old music-hall songs, courtesy of you-know-who. I think the first one I learned was 'Don't jump off the roof, Dad' ('You'll make a hole in the yard!'). I have so many recollections of shows she and I would put on for my parents, my grandfather, the dog … anyone who would watch, really. Sometimes we'd just put on shows because it was fun, and no one had to watch at all. What happy, happy times! It was also the trip where she told me about Mr and Mrs Pepperpot and made me a part of the story by telling me of some very special party shoes, which were hidden behind a certain tree. And of course there really were shoes there. And I wore them out.

It is difficult for me to pick and choose snapshots from the past. There are so many, but I can hardly write about Dame Thora Hird without writing about her fondness for egg custard. I don't recall how it began, but it is very important! From shouting 'Egg custard!' and diving into the depths of the most fluffy duvet of all time, to incorporating it in a poem – which both of us do each birthday, Christmas, Easter and so on – to actually eating it, it is one of those little 'inside' things you have in a family that starts off silly, continues to be silly, and grows into time-honoured tradition.

I admire her so much, her wit, her brains, her tremendous talent, her storytelling both on and off the screen. She's one of a kind, all right. Watching me ride a bike for the first time in the mews with my grandfather, Papa, who taught me! Telling me little industry secrets and idiosyncrasies, like how she would always like to sign contracts on Fridays if she could. Dressing me up for birthday parties, taking me to see *The Mousetrap* and then going to Roules for a late supper afterwards. Introducing me to and getting me hooked on crosswords. I'm thankful, I'm lucky, and like she says, 'Blood is thicker than dip!'

Thora feeding granddaughter Daisy in 1971 – on one of the many trips she and Scottie made to the USA to visit the family.

Scottie and Thora on a sight-seeing trip in California with Janette and baby Daisy in 1972.

An early 1970s snapshot of American hit singer Mel Tormé holding baby Daisy, surrounded by Scottie, Janette and Thora, in the garden at the family's Beverly Hills home.

JAMES TORMÉ

One of the really cool things about having a famous and respected gran is that you never have to worry about running out of things to say. In fact, when we have a yak, there is never enough time to talk about everything that's happening. Everything that's happening to her. Here's a woman who can talk about (in extreme detail) the recent or not-so-recent past, the present or the future in a way that simply captivates a person's curiosity, and then has them believing that the story they're hearing is the only important information anywhere! This narrator holds on to stories, and details within those stories, that the rest of us have long since dismissed as trivial and unimportant. These same stories and details have remained effervescing on the surface of her conscience, bubbling beneath the surface of her grey matter – to be repeated sometimes decades later in order to highlight a symbolic importance which everyone else has long lost the power to recognise.

Notwithstanding, what really does blow my mind is that my gran, who was endowed with an extraordinary abundance of skill and intensity, also has an unlimited capacity to care for other human beings. She lives her life expressing a uniquely warm brand of love and concern for fellow men and women. It would appear that years of being loved so universally has spawned the capacity to love outwardly beyond normal expectations. Or maybe she was simply always grounded in wisdom and empathy of this type. Either way, it's hard to believe and a joy to behold.

It was an intense honour and proud moment for me when the Queen knighted my gran at Buckingham Palace. Although it was a moment I shall never forget, it cannot compare, in any way, to the privilege of being honoured – showered if you will – by the love which radiates from her heart to mine, grandmother to grandson. My gran!

Now let's revise: her name is Dame Thora Hird OBE, D.Lit. And don't you forget it. I promise you she wouldn't forget yours!

Praise be! (AT THE MILL HOUSE)

You've heard the saying, 'third time lucky'? Well, that certainly seems to have been the case for my Jan. After being married twice, when sadly both relationships didn't work out, she met William back in the late 1970s. They seemed to hit it off straightaway, but Scottie and I didn't want to get our hopes up too high after Jan's difficult experiences in the past.

Thankfully, things did work out and they married in 1981 and have been together ever since. And I am so happy for them because they love each other so much.

William already had four children when he met Jan, and she had two, so they needed a big house to move into. They bought a lovely old house, big enough for all of them, called the Mill House, at Isfield. It had several acres, a wood, two meadows and a river running through it. If that starts to sound familiar to you, that's because for many years it became the setting for the filming of *Praise Be!*

Originally, the production team were supposed to use only a living-room in the grand house, but slowly, as the director saw more of the house and the

Thora at her country cottage, next door to her
daughter Janette, in Chichester.

In the living-room of the
Mill House at Isfield,
grandson James and
granddaughter Daisy join
Thora, Jan and Scottie for
the filming of another
episode of the BBC religious
programme, *Praise Be!*

JANETTE SCOTT

Mum had been presenting *Praise Be!* for BBC TV every Sunday for many years when I returned
to live in England in 1981. My husband, Daisy, James and I lived in East Sussex in a home
called the Mill House, with seventeen acres and various outbuildings such as stables, a barn
and a small cottage that was ideal for Mum and Dad as a weekend hideaway. My parents
worked hard on the garden and the cottage and made it delightful.

I can't remember how it happened, but shortly after we moved in, one of the *Praise Be!*
programmes was filmed away from the TV studios, on location in the living-room of my home.
It worked so well and it was so beautifully easy for Mum to walk over from the cottage to the
main house that the next season the entire series was filmed there. In following seasons the
production ventured beyond the confines of the living-room to include the dining-room, the
snug, the kitchen, the front door and hallway, and the conservatory. The grounds too were shot
from every conceivable angle; the river bank, the orchard, the rose garden, the greenhouse and
vegetable garden. Featured players were our Muscovy ducks and the wild mallards, the geese
and our rare breed of chickens. Stars of the show were often Lucy, our Californian Cocker
spaniel; Jess, our Labrador, and her daughter, Patch. I would stand behind Mother out of
camera view, and hold dog treats up high so that the dogs appear to be totally absorbed with
Mother's tales of St Francis and the Bible stories. We looked forward to being 'taken over' by
the film crew each season. Writer/director Liz Barr and producer Valletta Stallabrass remain
close family friends to this day.

adjoining grounds, she asked if we would mind them filming a little more here and there. In the end, you could have cut together an episode of *Through the Keyhole*, you'd seen so much of the place, though you didn't need to guess who was living there.

We went back to the Mill House for one week every year to record the links for the shows, and Jan was so patient as we filled up her hall with cables and groundsheets. Mind you, the family did get a chance to appear on the shows, even Daisy and James who could only have been about ten and eight at the time. It was a happy home and a very happy time for us all.

Dance Practice

You would imagine, wouldn't you, that with both my daughter Jan and myself being such busy actresses working on so many films in the 1950s we would have worked together more often than we did? When I say 'worked together' I actually mean appearing in scenes together, because there were times when we were both cast in the same film but did not actually meet on screen.

I remember two films we both made in the mid-1950s. In the first, *Now and Forever*, my part was so small that I'm not sure I even got a credit for it. Jan took the lead role as a lonely schoolgirl who plans to elope and is then chased across the country by two sets of parents. I played the maid, and Jan and I shared a very brief scene together.

Our next film was *The Good Companions*, also made at Elstree, about a group of ill-assorted youths taking to the road and joining a dancing troupe. Jan had to work hard on her dancing skills for that one and she spent hours and hours in our garage at our mews home in London with her dancing instructor until she got her steps just right.

Forty years later, *Last of the Summer Wine* producer Alan J. W. Bell allowed us to work together again – well, appear in the same episode anyway – when he sat Jan in the church as an 'extra' in the 1997 Christmas Special, 'There Goes the Groom'. He tried to entice her back to acting by offering 'speaking' appearances in the series, but Jan politely refused.

I've mentioned before that we now film the interiors for *Summer Wine* at a studio before playing them to an audience to pick up their laughter for the soundtrack. A few years back we filmed at Elstree Studios. It was wonderful to be back there after so many years, filming on the very same stages I had filmed on some forty years previously.

It looks great fun but six months of intense dance training was called for when Janette landed a lead role in the musical *The Good Companions*. Here she can be seen rehearsing in Thora's garage at their London home.

JANETTE SCOTT

When film producer/director Mario Zampi cast me as the female lead in the film *Now and Forever*, he asked Mum to test for the part of my mother in the film. She laughed and said: 'You need someone good-looking to play Jan's mother! No one would believe me in that role.' So Mario then offered her a cameo role as the part of the maid, which she accepted with great pleasure.

The next year, Mother and I worked together again, though my preparation for the role was far more demanding. It was 1955 and Associated British Pictures were preparing to film *The Good Companions* at Elstree Studios. My role demanded lots of dancing and so my usual dance training had to be intensified. Apart from ballet classes three times a week and tap lessons twice a week, Jack Billings, the dancer and choreographer, was sent to the mews house every weekday morning for six months to prepare me to be handed over to Paddy Stone and Riving Davies for the musical numbers in the film. Dad had already converted the garage into a rehearsal hall for me, with ballet barres and mirrors. He then added speakers for the music to be piped downstairs for us to be able to rehearse properly.

Film producer/ director Mario Zampi on the set of *Now and Forever* in 1955, one of the few occasions that mother and daughter appeared on screen together.

Fellowship from the University of Central Lancashire

A proud mother with an even prouder daughter, as Thora and Janette celebrate an honorary fellowship from the University of Central Lancashire in November 2000

I was so proud to be awarded an honorary fellowship by the University of Central Lancashire. They call it 'honorary'. Well, I can tell you it was certainly an honour for me.

The ceremony took place in Lancaster itself next to what used to be the old Town Hall. Now that brings back a funny memory. I say funny, but it wasn't at the time.

I've always enjoyed dressing up for special occasions and one night, back in the 1920s it was, I had a ticket for the Co-op Dinner Dance at Lancaster Town Hall. Price 2/6d (two shillings and sixpence) all in. I was thrilled to bits with my new, pale-green satin dress with its 7-inch, georgette, 'handkerchief' pointed hemline. Doris Brown, our neighbour, had made it for me and done a grand job. I wore brocade shoes and my hair was done up in 'earphones' (that's when your hair is braided, then wound round into saucer shapes over your ears … get it?). White kid gloves and a small evening bag – containing lipstick, powder compact and lace-edged hanky – completed the picture.

We took our places for dinner, and as the waiter started to put a bowl of mushroom soup in front of me, he caught his elbow on the back of the chair of the person sitting next to me. Whoops! The entire portion of soup tipped straight on to my lap. I yelled. It was hot and already soaking through the dress and my pure silk stockings. Peg, my best friend, and I rushed off to the ladies' toilet.

Now, I know I write of the good old days a great deal, but in the 1920s ladies' rooms weren't half as good as they are today. No boxes of tissues, no paper towels, no machines blowing hot air – nothing except a small roller towel hung up so high that I could only reach the bottom two or three inches. It was impossible to wipe the dress without taking it off, over the 'earphones'. By now the tears were very near. We wiped the dress with our lace hankies, I put it back on and I returned to the table crumpled and wet. Everyone was very sympathetic, of course.

Later, a young man asked me to dance. I thanked him, saying I couldn't dance with a wet frock. 'I'm not a wet frock,' he replied. There's always a comic to hand in Lancashire.

I didn't mention all this when I received my fellowship, though I did have to hold back a smile as the memories came flooding back that day.

Number Ten, Downing Street

I've had the privilege of meeting three Prime Ministers at 10 Downing Street. The first was Margaret Thatcher, back in April 1989. I had been to a special Spring service at the Methodist Central Hall at Westminster to celebrate new life – Daffodil Day we call it – and Scottie and I walked up Downing Street with some flowers under our arms. A kind secretary took them from us and put them in water. We talked, the Prime Minister and I, about our busy lives and I was very impressed when she told me that she wrote her 'thank you' notes on the same day she received things, even if she had been through a long day of engagements. Scottie and I remarked afterwards how nice it was to see her as proud as any woman would be of showing us her special home.

A few years later John and Norma Major invited me for a summer's evening garden party. I was a little disappointed by the gardens – not many flowers – but not at all disappointed by the Majors. They are a wonderful and genuine couple, and I did feel sorry that John Major seemed to have such a troubled time during his years in office. Some people said he was too kind for the job. He was certainly very kind to me and commented on the Union Jack brooch that I wore that night.

Ten years after my first visit to Downing Street, I was back there again for a reception on behalf of the Stroke Association. This time I was welcomed by Tony and Cherie Blair. The place had been redecorated and though it looked very different from my first visit, it was obvious that Cherie had taken great pride in overseeing the changes.

Tony Blair arrived late – he had been at the TUC Conference in Brighton – and when he saw me he came over for a chat. Many people don't realise that his father Leo had a stroke when Tony was just nine years old. It was three years before his father spoke again. Tony said it changes the life not just of the person who has the stroke but also of everyone around them. Oh, how I know that to be true! My dear Scottie died from a stroke. So Jan and I both understood what he meant.

It's that man! Thora – escorted by daughter Jan – on her third visit to 10 Downing Street, where she met up with Prime Minister Tony Blair at a reception in aid of the Stroke Association.